The Spanish Student by Henry Wadsworth Longfellow

Henry Wadsworth Longfellow was born on February 27th, 1807 in Portland, Maine. As a young boy, it was obvious that he was very studious and he quickly became fluent in Latin.

He published his first poem, "The Battle of Lovell's Pond", in the Portland Gazette on November 17th, 1820. He was already thinking of a career in literature and, in his senior year, wrote to his father: "I will not disguise it in the least... the fact is, I most eagerly aspire after future eminence in literature, my whole soul burns most ardently after it, and every earthly thought centers in it...."

After graduation travels in Europe occupied the next three years and he seemed to easily absorb any language he set himself to learn.

On September 14th, 1831, Longfellow married Mary Storer Potter. They settled in Brunswick.

His first published book was in 1833, a translation of poems by the Spanish poet Jorge Manrique. He also published a travel book, Outre-Mer: A Pilgrimage Beyond the Sea.

During a trip to Europe Mary became pregnant. Sadly, in October 1835, she miscarried at some six months. After weeks of illness she died, at the age of 22 on November 29th, 1835. Longfellow wrote "One thought occupies me night and day... She is dead — She is dead! All day I am weary and sad".

In late 1839, Longfellow published Hyperion, a book in prose inspired by his trips abroad.

Ballads and Other Poems was published in 1841 and included "The Village Blacksmith" and "The Wreck of the Hesperus". His reputation as a poet, and a commercial one at that, was set.

On May 10th, 1843, after seven years in pursuit of a chance for new love, Longfellow received word from Fanny Appleton that she agreed to marry him.

On November 1st, 1847, the epic poem Evangeline was published.

In 1854, Longfellow retired from Harvard, to devote himself entirely to writing.

The Song of Haiwatha, perhaps his best known and enjoyed work was published in 1855.

On July 10th, 1861, after suffering horrific burns the previous day. In his attempts to save her Longfellow had also been badly burned and was unable to attend her funeral.

He spent several years translating Dante Alighieri's Divine Comedy. It was published in 1867.

Longfellow was also part of a group who became known as The Fireside Poets which also included William Cullen Bryant, John Greenleaf Whittier, James Russell Lowell, and Oliver Wendell Holmes Snr.

Longfellow was the most popular poet of his day. As a friend once wrote to him, "no other poet was so fully recognized in his lifetime". Some of his works including "Paul Revere's Ride" and "The Song of Haiwatha" may have rewritten the facts but became essential parts of the American psyche and culture.

Henry Wadsworth Longfellow died, surrounded by family, on Friday, March 24th, 1882. He had been suffering from peritonitis.

Index of Contents

DRAMATIS PERSONAE

VICTORIAN	}
HYPOLITO	}Students of Alcala.

THE COUNT OF LARA	}
DON CARLOS	}Gentlemen of Madrid.

THE ARCHBISHOP OF TOLEDO.
A CARDINAL.

BELTRAN CRUZADO	Count of the Gypsies.
BARTOLOME ROMAN	A young Gypsy.
PADRE CURA OF GUADARRAMA	
PEDRO CRESPO	Alcalde.
PANCHO	Alguacil.
FRANCISCO	Lara's Servant.
CHISPA	Victorian's Servant.
BALTASAR	Innkeeper.
PRECIOSA	A Gypsy Girl.
ANGELICA	A poor Girl.
MARTINA	The Padre Cura's Niece.
DOLORES	Preciosa's Maid.
Gypsies, Musicians, etc.	

ACT I

SCENE I.—The Count of Lara's Chambers. Night.

The **COUNT of LARA** in his dressing-gown, smoking and conversing with **DON CARLOS**.

COUNT of LARA
You were not at the play tonight, Don Carlos;
How happened it?

DON CARLOS
I had engagements elsewhere.
Pray who was there?

COUNT of LARA
Why all the town and court.
The house was crowded; and the busy fans
Among the gayly dressed and perfumed ladies
Fluttered like butterflies among the flowers.
There was the Countess of Medina Celi;
The Goblin Lady with her Phantom Lover,
Her Lindo Don Diego; Dona Sol;
And Dona Serafina, and her cousins.

DON CARLOS
What was the play?

COUNT of LARA
It was a dull affair;
One of those comedies in which you see,
As Lope says, the history of the world
Brought down from Genesis to the Day of Judgment.

There were three duels fought in the first act,
Three gentlemen receiving deadly wounds,
Laying their hands upon their hearts, and saying,
"O, I am dead!" a lover in a closet,
An old hidalgo, and a gay Don Juan,
A Dona Inez with a black mantilla,
Followed at twilight by an unknown lover,
Who looks intently where he knows she is not!

DON CARLOS
Of course, the Preciosa danced to-night?

COUNT of LARA
And never better. Every footstep fell
As lightly as a sunbeam on the water.
I think the girl extremely beautiful.

DON CARLOS
Almost beyond the privilege of woman!
I saw her in the Prado yesterday.
Her step was royal,—queen-like,—and her face
As beautiful as a saint's in Paradise.

COUNT of LARA
May not a saint fall from her Paradise,
And be no more a saint?

DON CARLOS
Why do you ask?

COUNT of LARA
Because I have heard it said this angel fell,
And though she is a virgin outwardly,
Within she is a sinner; like those panels
Of doors and altar-pieces the old monks
Painted in convents, with the Virgin Mary
On the outside, and on the inside Venus!

DON CARLOS
You do her wrong; indeed, you do her wrong!
She is as virtuous as she is fair.

COUNT of LARA
How credulous you are! Why look you, friend,
There's not a virtuous woman in Madrid,
In this whole city! And would you persuade me
That a mere dancing-girl, who shows herself,
Nightly, half naked, on the stage, for money,

And with voluptuous motions fires the blood
Of inconsiderate youth, is to be held
A model for her virtue?

DON CARLOS
You forget
She is a Gypsy girl.

COUNT of LARA
And therefore won
The easier.

DON CARLOS
Nay, not to be won at all!
The only virtue that a Gypsy prizes
Is chastity. That is her only virtue.
Dearer than life she holds it. I remember
A Gypsy woman, a vile, shameless bawd,
Whose craft was to betray the young and fair;
And yet this woman was above all bribes.
And when a noble lord, touched by her beauty,
The wild and wizard beauty of her race,
Offered her gold to be what she made others,
She turned upon him, with a look of scorn,
And smote him in the face!

COUNT of LARA
And does that prove
That Preciosa is above suspicion?

DON CARLOS
It proves a nobleman may be repulsed
When he thinks conquest easy. I believe
That woman, in her deepest degradation,
Holds something sacred, something undefiled,
Some pledge and keepsake of her higher nature,
And, like the diamond in the dark, retains
Some quenchless gleam of the celestial light!

COUNT of LARA
Yet Preciosa would have taken the gold.

DON CARLOS [Rising]
I do not think so.

COUNT of LARA
I am sure of it.
But why this haste? Stay yet a little longer,

And fight the battles of your Dulcinea.

DON CARLOS
'T is late. I must begone, for if I stay
You will not be persuaded.

COUNT of LARA
Yes; persuade me.

DON CARLOS
No one so deaf as he who will not hear!

COUNT of LARA
No one so blind as he who will not see!

DON CARLOS
And so good night. I wish you pleasant dreams,
And greater faith in woman.

[Exit.

COUNT of LARA
Greater faith!
I have the greatest faith; for I believe
Victorian is her lover. I believe
That I shall be to-morrow; and thereafter
Another, and another, and another,
Chasing each other through her zodiac,
As Taurus chases Aries.

[Enter **FRANCISCO** with a casket.

Well, Francisco,
What speed with Preciosa?

FRANCISCO
None, my lord.
She sends your jewels back, and bids me tell you
She is not to be purchased by your gold.

COUNT of LARA
Then I will try some other way to win her.
Pray, dost thou know Victorian?

FRANCISCO
Yes, my lord;
I saw him at the jeweller's to-day.

COUNT of LARA
What was he doing there?

FRANCISCO
I saw him buy
A golden ring, that had a ruby in it.

COUNT of LARA
Was there another like it?

FRANCISCO
One so like it
I could not choose between them.

COUNT of LARA
It is well.
To-morrow morning bring that ring to me.
Do not forget. Now light me to my bed.

[Exeunt.

SCENE II. — A Street in Madrid

Enter **CHISPA**, followed by **MUSICIANS**, with a bagpipe, guitars, and other instruments.

CHISPA
Abernuncio Satanas! and a plague on all lovers who ramble about at night, drinking the elements, instead of sleeping quietly in their beds. Every dead man to his cemetery, say I; and every friar to his monastery. Now, here's my master, Victorian, yesterday a cow-keeper, and to-day a gentleman; yesterday a student, and to-day a lover; and I must be up later than the nightingale, for as the abbot sings so must the sacristan respond. God grant he may soon be married, for then shall all this serenading cease. Ay, marry! marry! marry! Mother, what does marry mean? It means to spin, to bear children, and to weep, my daughter! And, of a truth, there is something more in matrimony than the wedding-ring.

[To the **MUSICIANS**] And now, gentlemen, Pax vobiscum! as the ass said to the cabbages. Pray, walk this way; and don't hang down your heads. It is no disgrace to have an old father and a ragged shirt. Now, look you, you are gentlemen who lead the life of crickets; you enjoy hunger by day and noise by night. Yet, I beseech you, for this once be not loud, but pathetic; for it is a serenade to a damsel in bed, and not to the Man in the Moon. Your object is not to arouse and terrify, but to soothe and bring lulling dreams. Therefore, each shall not play upon his instrument as if it were the only one in the universe, but gently, and with a certain modesty, according with the others. Pray, how may I call thy name, friend?

FIRST MUSICIAN
Geronimo Gil, at your service.

CHISPA

Every tub smells of the wine that is in it. Pray, Geronimo, is not Saturday an unpleasant day with thee?

FIRST MUSICIAN

Why so?

CHISPA

Because I have heard it said that Saturday is an unpleasant day with those who have but one shirt. Moreover, I have seen thee at the tavern, and if thou canst run as fast as thou canst drink, I should like to hunt hares with thee. What instrument is that?

FIRST MUSICIAN

An Aragonese bagpipe.

CHISPA

Pray, art thou related to the bagpiper of Bujalance, who asked a maravedi for playing, and ten for leaving off?

FIRST MUSICIAN

No, your honor.

CHISPA

I am glad of it. What other instruments have we?

SECOND & THIRD MUSICIAN

We play the bandurria.

CHISPA

A pleasing instrument. And thou?

FOURTH MUSICIAN

The fife.

CHISPA

I like it; it has a cheerful, soul-stirring sound, that soars up to my lady's window like the song of a swallow. And you others?

OTHER MUSICIANS

We are the singers, please your honor.

CHISPA

You are too many. Do you think we are going to sing mass in the cathedral of Cordova? Four men can make but little use of one shoe, and I see not how you can all sing in one song. But follow me along the garden wall. That is the way my master climbs to the lady's window, it is by the Vicar's skirts that the Devil climbs into the belfry. Come, follow me, and make no noise.

[Exeunt.

She stands at the open window.

PRECIOSA
How slowly through the lilac-scented air
Descends the tranquil moon! Like thistle-down
The vapory clouds float in the peaceful sky;
And sweetly from yon hollow vaults of shade
The nightingales breathe out their souls in song.
And hark! what songs of love, what soul-like sounds,
Answer them from below!

SERENADE.

Stars of the summer night!
Far in yon azure deeps,
Hide, hide your golden light!
She sleeps!
My lady sleeps!
Sleeps!

Moon of the summer night!
Far down yon western steeps,
Sink, sink in silver light!
She sleeps!
My lady sleeps!
Sleeps!

Wind of the summer night!
Where yonder woodbine creeps,
Fold, fold thy pinions light!
She sleeps!
My lady sleeps!
Sleeps!

Dreams of the summer night!
Tell her, her lover keeps
Watch! while in slumbers light
She sleeps
My lady sleeps
Sleeps!

[Enter **VICTORIAN** by the balcony.

VICTORIAN

Poor little dove! Thou tremblest like a leaf!

PRECIOSA

I am so frightened! 'T is for thee I tremble!
I hate to have thee climb that wall by night!
Did no one see thee?

VICTORIAN

None, my love, but thou.

PRECIOSA

'T is very dangerous; and when thou art gone
I chide myself for letting thee come here
Thus stealthily by night. Where hast thou been?
Since yesterday I have no news from thee.

VICTORIAN

Since yesterday I have been in Alcala.
Erelong the time will come, sweet Preciosa,
When that dull distance shall no more divide us;
And I no more shall scale thy wall by night
To steal a kiss from thee, as I do now.

PRECIOSA

An honest thief, to steal but what thou givest.

VICTORIAN

And we shall sit together unmolested,
And words of true love pass from tongue to tongue,
As singing birds from one bough to another.

PRECIOSA

That were a life to make time envious!
I knew that thou wouldst come to me to-night.
I saw thee at the play.

VICTORIAN

Sweet child of air!
Never did I behold thee so attired
And garmented in beauty as to-night!
What hast thou done to make thee look so fair?

PRECIOSA

Am I not always fair?

VICTORIAN

Ay, and so fair

That I am jealous of all eyes that see thee,
And wish that they were blind.

PRECIOSA
I heed them not;
When thou art present, I see none but thee!

VICTORIAN
There's nothing fair nor beautiful, but takes
Something from thee, that makes it beautiful.

PRECIOSA
And yet thou leavest me for those dusty books.

VICTORIAN
Thou comest between me and those books too often!
I see thy face in everything I see!
The paintings in the chapel wear thy looks,
The canticles are changed to sarabands,
And with the leaned doctors of the schools
I see thee dance cachuchas.

PRECIOSA
In good sooth,
I dance with learned doctors of the schools
To-morrow morning.

VICTORIAN
And with whom, I pray?

PRECIOSA
A grave and reverend Cardinal, and his Grace
The Archbishop of Toledo.

VICTORIAN
What mad jest
Is this?

PRECIOSA
It is no jest; indeed it is not.

VICTORIAN
Prithee, explain thyself.

PRECIOSA
Why, simply thus.
Thou knowest the Pope has sent here into Spain
To put a stop to dances on the stage.

VICTORIAN
I have heard it whispered.

PRECIOSA
Now the Cardinal,
Who for this purpose comes, would fain behold
With his own eyes these dances; and the Archbishop
Has sent for me—

VICTORIAN
That thou mayst dance before them!
Now viva la cachucha! It will breathe
The fire of youth into these gray old men!
'T will be thy proudest conquest!

PRECIOSA
Saving one.
And yet I fear these dances will be stopped,
And Preciosa be once more a beggar.

VICTORIAN
The sweetest beggar that e'er asked for alms;
With such beseeching eyes, that when I saw thee
I gave my heart away!

PRECIOSA
Dost thou remember
When first we met?

VICTORIAN
It was at Cordova,
In the cathedral garden. Thou wast sitting
Under the orange-trees, beside a fountain.

PRECIOSA
'T was Easter-Sunday. The full-blossomed trees
Filled all the air with fragrance and with joy.
The priests were singing, and the organ sounded,
And then anon the great cathedral bell.
It was the elevation of the Host.
We both of us fell down upon our knees,
Under the orange boughs, and prayed together.
I never had been happy till that moment.

VICTORIAN
Thou blessed angel!

PRECIOSA

And when thou wast gone
I felt an acting here. I did not speak
To any one that day. But from that day
Bartolome grew hateful unto me.

VICTORIAN

Remember him no more. Let not his shadow
Come between thee and me. Sweet Preciosa!
I loved thee even then, though I was silent!

PRECIOSA

I thought I ne'er should see thy face again.
Thy farewell had a sound of sorrow in it.

VICTORIAN

That was the first sound in the song of love!
Scarce more than silence is, and yet a sound.
Hands of invisible spirits touch the strings
Of that mysterious instrument, the soul,
And play the prelude of our fate. We hear
The voice prophetic, and are not alone.

PRECIOSA

That is my faith. Dust thou believe these warnings?

VICTORIAN

So far as this. Our feelings and our thoughts
Tend ever on, and rest not in the Present.
As drops of rain fall into some dark well,
And from below comes a scarce audible sound,
So fall our thoughts into the dark Hereafter,
And their mysterious echo reaches us.

PRECIOSA

I have felt it so, but found no words to say it!
I cannot reason; I can only feel!
But thou hast language for all thoughts and feelings.
Thou art a scholar; and sometimes I think
We cannot walk together in this world!
The distance that divides us is too great!
Henceforth thy pathway lies among the stars;
I must not hold thee back.

VICTORIAN

Thou little sceptic!
Dost thou still doubt? What I most prize in woman
Is her affections, not her intellect!

The intellect is finite; but the affections
Are infinite, and cannot be exhausted.
Compare me with the great men of the earth;
What am I? Why, a pygmy among giants!
But if thou lovest,—mark me! I say lovest,
The greatest of thy sex excels thee not!
The world of the affections is thy world,
Not that of man's ambition. In that stillness
Which most becomes a woman, calm and holy,
Thou sittest by the fireside of the heart,
Feeding its flame. The element of fire
Is pure. It cannot change nor hide its nature,
But burns as brightly in a Gypsy camp
As in a palace hall. Art thou convinced?

PRECIOSA
Yes, that I love thee, as the good love heaven;
But not that I am worthy of that heaven.
How shall I more deserve it?

VICTORIAN
Loving more.

PRECIOSA
I cannot love thee more; my heart is full.

VICTORIAN
Then let it overflow, and I will drink it,
As in the summer-time the thirsty sands
Drink the swift waters of the Manzanares,
And still do thirst for more.

A WATCHMAN [In the street]
Ave Maria
Purissima! 'T is midnight and serene!

VICTORIAN
Hear'st thou that cry?

PRECIOSA
It is a hateful sound,
To scare thee from me!

VICTORIAN
As the hunter's horn
Doth scare the timid stag, or bark of hounds
The moor-fowl from his mate.

PRECIOSA
Pray, do not go!

VICTORIAN
I must away to Alcala to-night.
Think of me when I am away.

PRECIOSA
Fear not!
I have no thoughts that do not think of thee.

VICTORIAN [Giving her a ring]
And to remind thee of my love, take this;
A serpent, emblem of Eternity;
A ruby,—say, a drop of my heart's blood.

PRECIOSA
It is an ancient saying, that the ruby
Brings gladness to the wearer, and preserves
The heart pure, and, if laid beneath the pillow,
Drives away evil dreams. But then, alas!
It was a serpent tempted Eve to sin.

VICTORIAN
What convent of barefooted Carmelites
Taught thee so much theology?

PRECIOSA [Laying her hand upon his mouth]
Hush! hush!
Good night! and may all holy angels guard thee!

VICTORIAN
Good night! good night! Thou art my guardian angel!
I have no other saint than thou to pray to!

[He descends by the balcony.

PRECIOSA
Take care, and do not hurt thee.
Art thou safe?

VICTORIAN [From the garden]
Safe as my love for thee! But art thou safe?
Others can climb a balcony by moonlight
As well as I. Pray shut thy window close;
I am jealous of the perfumed air of night
That from this garden climbs to kiss thy lips.

PRECIOSA [Throwing down her handkerchief]
Thou silly child! Take this to blind thine eyes.
It is my benison!

VICTORIAN
And brings to me
Sweet fragrance from thy lips, as the soft wind
Wafts to the out-bound mariner the breath
Of the beloved land he leaves behind.

PRECIOSA
Make not thy voyage long.

VICTORIAN
To-morrow night
Shall see me safe returned. Thou art the star
To guide me to an anchorage. Good night!
My beauteous star! My star of love, good night!

PRECIOSA
Good night!

WATCHMAN [At a distance]
Ave Maria Purissima!

SCENE IV. — An Inn on the Road to Alcala

BALTASAR asleep on a bench. Enter **CHISPA**.

CHISPA
And here we are, halfway to Alcala, between cocks and midnight. Body o' me! what an inn this is! The lights out, and the landlord asleep. Hola! ancient Baltasar!

BALTASAR [Waking]
Here I am.

CHISPA
Yes, there you are, like a one-eyed Alcalde in a town without inhabitants. Bring a light, and let me have supper.

BALTASAR
Where is your master?

CHISPA
Do not trouble yourself about him. We have stopped a moment to breathe our horses; and, if he chooses to walk up and down in the open air, looking into the sky as one who hears it rain, that does not

satisfy my hunger, you know. But be quick, for I am in a hurry, and every man stretches his legs according to the length of his coverlet. What have we here?

BALTASAR [Setting a light on the table]
Stewed rabbit.

CHISPA [Eating]
Conscience of Portalegre! Stewed kitten, you mean!

BALTASAR
And a pitcher of Pedro Ximenes, with a roasted pear in it.

CHISPA [Drinking]
Ancient Baltasar, amigo! You know how to cry wine and sell vinegar. I tell you this is nothing but Vino Tinto of La Mancha, with a tang of the swine-skin.

BALTASAR
I swear to you by Saint Simon and Judas, it is all as I say.

CHISPA
And I swear to you by Saint Peter and Saint Paul, that it is no such thing. Moreover, your supper is like the hidalgo's dinner, very little meat and a great deal of tablecloth.

BALTASAR
Ha! ha! ha!

CHISPA
And more noise than nuts.

BALTASAR
Ha! ha! ha! You must have your joke, Master Chispa.
But shall I not ask Don Victorian in, to take a draught of the Pedro Ximenes?

CHISPA
No; you might as well say, "Don't-you-want-some?" to a dead man.

BALTASAR
Why does he go so often to Madrid?

CHISPA
For the same reason that he eats no supper. He is in love. Were you ever in love, Baltasar?

BALTASAR
I was never out of it, good Chispa. It has been the torment of my life.

CHISPA
What! are you on fire, too, old hay-stack? Why, we shall never be able to put you out.

VICTORIAN [Without]
Chispa!

CHISPA
Go to bed, Pero Grullo, for the cocks are crowing.

VICTORIAN
Ea! Chispa! Chispa!

CHISPA
Ea! Senor. Come with me, ancient Baltasar, and bring water for the horses. I will pay for the supper tomorrow.

[Exeunt.

SCENE V. – Victorian's Chambers at Alcala.

HYPOLITO asleep in an arm-chair. He awakes slowly.

HYPOLITO
I must have been asleep! ay, sound asleep!
And it was all a dream. O sleep, sweet sleep
Whatever form thou takest, thou art fair,
Holding unto our lips thy goblet filled
Out of Oblivion's well, a healing draught!
The candles have burned low; it must be late.
Where can Victorian be? Like Fray Carrillo,
The only place in which one cannot find him
Is his own cell. Here's his guitar, that seldom
Feels the caresses of its master's hand.
Open thy silent lips, sweet instrument!
And make dull midnight merry with a song.

[He plays and sings.

Padre Francisco!
Padre Francisco!
What do you want of Padre Francisco?
Here is a pretty young maiden
Who wants to confess her sins!
Open the door and let her come in,
I will shrive her from every sin.

[Enter **VICTORIAN**]

VICTORIAN

Padre Hypolito! Padre Hypolito!

HYPOLITO
What do you want of Padre Hypolito?

VICTORIAN
Come, shrive me straight; for, if love be a sin,
I am the greatest sinner that doth live.
I will confess the sweetest of all crimes,
A maiden wooed and won.

HYPOLITO
The same old tale
Of the old woman in the chimney-corner,
Who, while the pot boils, says, "Come here, my child;
I'll tell thee a story of my wedding-day."

VICTORIAN
Nay, listen, for my heart is full; so full
That I must speak.

HYPOLITO
Alas! that heart of thine
Is like a scene in the old play; the curtain
Rises to solemn music, and lo! enter
The eleven thousand virgins of Cologne!

VICTORIAN
Nay, like the Sibyl's volumes, thou shouldst say;
Those that remained, after the six were burned,
Being held more precious than the nine together.
But listen to my tale. Dost thou remember
The Gypsy girl we saw at Cordova
Dance the Romalis in the market-place?

HYPOLITO
Thou meanest Preciosa.

VICTORIAN
Ay, the same.
Thou knowest how her image haunted me
Long after we returned to Alcala.
She's in Madrid.

HYPOLITO
I know it.

VICTORIAN

And I'm in love.

HYPOLITO
And therefore in Madrid when thou shouldst be
In Alcala.

VICTORIAN
O pardon me, my friend,
If I so long have kept this secret from thee;
But silence is the charm that guards such treasures,
And, if a word be spoken ere the time,
They sink again, they were not meant for us.

HYPOLITO
Alas! alas! I see thou art in love.
Love keeps the cold out better than a cloak.
It serves for food and raiment. Give a Spaniard
His mass, his olla, and his Dona Luisa—
Thou knowest the proverb. But pray tell me, lover,
How speeds thy wooing? Is the maiden coy?
Write her a song, beginning with an Ave;
Sing as the monk sang to the Virgin Mary,

Ave! cujus calcem clare
Nec centenni commendare
Sciret Seraph studio!

VICTORIAN
Pray, do not jest! This is no time for it!
I am in earnest!

HYPOLITO
Seriously enamored?
What, ho! The Primus of great Alcala
Enamored of a Gypsy? Tell me frankly,
How meanest thou?

VICTORIAN
I mean it honestly.

HYPOLITO
Surely thou wilt not marry her!

VICTORIAN
Why not?

HYPOLITO
She was betrothed to one Bartolome,

If I remember rightly, a young Gypsy
Who danced with her at Cordova.

VICTORIAN
They quarrelled,
And so the matter ended.

HYPOLITO
But in truth
Thou wilt not marry her.

VICTORIAN
In truth I will.
The angels sang in heaven when she was born!
She is a precious jewel I have found
Among the filth and rubbish of the world.
I'll stoop for it; but when I wear it here,
Set on my forehead like the morning star,
The world may wonder, but it will not laugh.

HYPOLITO
If thou wear'st nothing else upon thy forehead,
'T will be indeed a wonder.

VICTORIAN
Out upon thee
With thy unseasonable jests! Pray tell me,
Is there no virtue in the world?

HYPOLITO
Not much.
What, think'st thou, is she doing at this moment;
Now, while we speak of her?

VICTORIAN
She lies asleep,
And from her parted lips her gentle breath
Comes like the fragrance from the lips of flowers.
Her tender limbs are still, and on her breast
The cross she prayed to, ere she fell asleep,
Rises and falls with the soft tide of dreams,
Like a light barge safe moored.

HYPOLITO
Which means, in prose,
She's sleeping with her mouth a little open!

VICTORIAN

O, would I had the old magician's glass
To see her as she lies in childlike sleep!

HYPOLITO
And wouldst thou venture?

VICTORIAN
Ay, indeed I would!

HYPOLITO
Thou art courageous. Hast thou e'er reflected
How much lies hidden in that one word, NOW?

VICTORIAN
Yes; all the awful mystery of Life!
I oft have thought, my dear Hypolito,
That could we, by some spell of magic, change
The world and its inhabitants to stone,
In the same attitudes they now are in,
What fearful glances downward might we cast
Into the hollow chasms of human life!
What groups should we behold about the death-bed,
Putting to shame the group of Niobe!
What joyful welcomes, and what sad farewells!
What stony tears in those congealed eyes!
What visible joy or anguish in those cheeks!
What bridal pomps, and what funereal shows!
What foes, like gladiators, fierce and struggling!
What lovers with their marble lips together!

HYPOLITO
Ay, there it is! and, if I were in love,
That is the very point I most should dread.
This magic glass, these magic spells of thine,
Might tell a tale were better left untold.
For instance, they might show us thy fair cousin,
The Lady Violante, bathed in tears
Of love and anger, like the maid of Colchis,
Whom thou, another faithless Argonaut,
Having won that golden fleece, a woman's love,
Desertest for this Glauce.

VICTORIAN
Hold thy peace!
She cares not for me. She may wed another,
Or go into a convent, and, thus dying,
Marry Achilles in the Elysian Fields.

HYPOLITO [Rising]
And so, good night! Good morning, I should say.

[Clock strikes three.

Hark! how the loud and ponderous mace of Time
Knocks at the golden portals of the day!
And so, once more, good night! We'll speak more largely
Of Preciosa when we meet again.
Get thee to bed, and the magician, Sleep,
Shall show her to thee, in his magic glass,
In all her loveliness. Good night!

[Exit.

VICTORIAN
Good night!
But not to bed; for I must read awhile.

[Throws himself into the arm-chair which **HYPOLITO** has left, and lays a large book open upon his knees.

Must read, or sit in revery and watch
The changing color of the waves that break
Upon the idle sea-shore of the mind!
Visions of Fame! that once did visit me,
Making night glorious with your smile, where are ye?
O, who shall give me, now that ye are gone,
Juices of those immortal plants that bloom
Upon Olympus, making us immortal?
Or teach me where that wondrous mandrake grows
Whose magic root, torn from the earth with groans,
At midnight hour, can scare the fiends away,
And make the mind prolific in its fancies!
I have the wish, but want the will, to act!
Souls of great men departed! Ye whose words
Have come to light from the swift river of Time,
Like Roman swords found in the Tagus' bed,
Where is the strength to wield the arms ye bore?
From the barred visor of Antiquity
Reflected shines the eternal light of Truth,
As from a mirror! All the means of action—
The shapeless masses, the materials—
Lie everywhere about us. What we need
Is the celestial fire to change the flint
Into transparent crystal, bright and clear.
That fire is genius! The rude peasant sits
At evening in his smoky cot, and draws
With charcoal uncouth figures on the wall.

The son of genius comes, foot-sore with travel,
And begs a shelter from the inclement night.
He takes the charcoal from the peasant's hand,
And, by the magic of his touch at once
Transfigured, all its hidden virtues shine,
And, in the eyes of the astonished clown,
It gleams a diamond! Even thus transformed,
Rude popular traditions and old tales
Shine as immortal poems, at the touch
Of some poor, houseless, homeless, wandering bard,
Who had but a night's lodging for his pains.
But there are brighter dreams than those of Fame,
Which are the dreams of Love! Out of the heart
Rises the bright ideal of these dreams,
As from some woodland fount a spirit rises
And sinks again into its silent deeps,
Ere the enamored knight can touch her robe!
'T is this ideal that the soul of man,
Like the enamored knight beside the fountain,
Waits for upon the margin of Life's stream;
Waits to behold her rise from the dark waters,
Clad in a mortal shape! Alas! how many
Must wait in vain! The stream flows evermore,
But from its silent deeps no spirit rises!
Yet I, born under a propitious star,
Have found the bright ideal of my dreams.
Yes! she is ever with me. I can feel,
Here, as I sit at midnight and alone,
Her gentle breathing! on my breast can feel
The pressure of her head! God's benison
Rest ever on it! Close those beauteous eyes,
Sweet Sleep! and all the flowers that bloom at night
With balmy lips breathe in her ears my name!

[Gradually sinks asleep.

ACT II

SCENE I. — Preciosa's Chamber. Morning

PRECIOSA and **ANGELICA**.

PRECIOSA
Why will you go so soon? Stay yet awhile.
The poor too often turn away unheard
From hearts that shut against them with a sound

That will be heard in heaven. Pray, tell me more
Of your adversities. Keep nothing from me.
What is your landlord's name?

ANGELICA
The Count of Lara.

PRECIOSA
The Count of Lara? O, beware that man!
Mistrust his pity,—hold no parley with him!
And rather die an outcast in the streets
Than touch his gold.

ANGELICA
You know him, then!

PRECIOSA
As much
As any woman may, and yet be pure.
As you would keep your name without a blemish,
Beware of him!

ANGELICA
Alas! what can I do?
I cannot choose my friends. Each word of kindness,
Come whence it may, is welcome to the poor.

PRECIOSA
Make me your friend. A girl so young and fair
Should have no friends but those of her own sex.
What is your name?

ANGELICA
Angelica.

PRECIOSA
That name
Was given you, that you might be an angel
To her who bore you! When your infant smile
Made her home Paradise, you were her angel.
O, be an angel still! She needs that smile.
So long as you are innocent, fear nothing.
No one can harm you! I am a poor girl,
Whom chance has taken from the public streets.
I have no other shield than mine own virtue.
That is the charm which has protected me!
Amid a thousand perils, I have worn it
Here on my heart! It is my guardian angel.

ANGELICA [Rising]
I thank you for this counsel, dearest lady.

PRECIOSA
Thank me by following it.

ANGELICA
Indeed I will.

PRECIOSA
Pray, do not go. I have much more to say.

ANGELICA
My mother is alone. I dare not leave her.

PRECIOSA
Some other time, then, when we meet again.
You must not go away with words alone.

[Gives her a purse.

Take this. Would it were more.

ANGELICA
I thank you, lady.

PRECIOSA
No thanks. To-morrow come to me again.
I dance to-night,—perhaps for the last time.
But what I gain, I promise shall be yours,
If that can save you from the Count of Lara.

ANGELICA
O, my dear lady! how shall I be grateful
For so much kindness?

PRECIOSA
I deserve no thanks,
Thank Heaven, not me.

ANGELICA
Both Heaven and you.

PRECIOSA
Farewell.
Remember that you come again tomorrow.

ANGELICA
I will. And may the Blessed Virgin guard you,
And all good angels.

[Exit.

PRECIOSA
May they guard thee too,
And all the poor; for they have need of angels.
Now bring me, dear Dolores, my basquina,
My richest maja dress,—my dancing dress,
And my most precious jewels! Make me look
Fairer than night e'er saw me! I've a prize
To win this day, worthy of Preciosa!

[Enter **BELTRAN CRUZADO**.

CRUZADO
Ave Maria!

PRECIOSA
O God! my evil genius!
What seekest thou here to-day?

CRUZADO
Thyself,—my child.

PRECIOSA
What is thy will with me?

CRUZADO
Gold! gold!

PRECIOSA
I gave thee yesterday; I have no more.

CRUZADO
The gold of the Busne,—give me his gold!

PRECIOSA
I gave the last in charity to-day.

CRUZADO
That is a foolish lie.

PRECIOSA
It is the truth.

CRUZADO

Curses upon thee! Thou art not my child!
Hast thou given gold away, and not to me?
Not to thy father? To whom, then?

PRECIOSA

To one
Who needs it more.

CRUZADO

No one can need it more.

PRECIOSA

Thou art not poor.

CRUZADO

What, I, who lurk about
In dismal suburbs and unwholesome lanes
I, who am housed worse than the galley slave;
I, who am fed worse than the kennelled hound;
I, who am clothed in rags,—Beltran Cruzado,—
Not poor!

PRECIOSA

Thou hast a stout heart and strong hands.
Thou canst supply thy wants; what wouldst thou more?

CRUZADO

The gold of the Busne! give me his gold!

PRECIOSA

Beltran Cruzado! hear me once for all.
I speak the truth. So long as I had gold,
I gave it to thee freely, at all times,
Never denied thee; never had a wish
But to fulfil thine own. Now go in peace!
Be merciful, be patient, and ere long
Thou shalt have more.

CRUZADO

And if I have it not,
Thou shalt no longer dwell here in rich chambers,
Wear silken dresses, feed on dainty food,
And live in idleness; but go with me,
Dance the Romalis in the public streets,
And wander wild again o'er field and fell;
For here we stay not long.

PRECIOSA
What! march again?

CRUZADO
Ay, with all speed. I hate the crowded town!
I cannot breathe shut up within its gates
Air,—I want air, and sunshine, and blue sky,
The feeling of the breeze upon my face,
The feeling of the turf beneath my feet,
And no walls but the far-off mountain-tops.
Then I am free and strong,—once more myself,
Beltran Cruzado, Count of the Cales!

PRECIOSA
God speed thee on thy march!—I cannot go.

CRUZADO
Remember who I am, and who thou art
Be silent and obey! Yet one thing more.
Bartolome Roman—

PRECIOSA [With emotion]
O, I beseech thee
If my obedience and blameless life,
If my humility and meek submission
In all things hitherto, can move in thee
One feeling of compassion; if thou art
Indeed my father, and canst trace in me
One look of her who bore me, or one tone
That doth remind thee of her, let it plead
In my behalf, who am a feeble girl,
Too feeble to resist, and do not force me
To wed that man! I am afraid of him!
I do not love him! On my knees I beg thee
To use no violence, nor do in haste
What cannot be undone!

CRUZADO
O child, child, child!
Thou hast betrayed thy secret, as a bird
Betrays her nest, by striving to conceal it.
I will not leave thee here in the great city
To be a grandee's mistress. Make thee ready
To go with us; and until then remember
A watchful eye is on thee.

[Exit.

PRECIOSA
Woe is me!
I have a strange misgiving in my heart!
But that one deed of charity I'll do,
Befall what may; they cannot take that from me.

SCENE II — A Room in the Archbishop's Palace

The **ARCHBISHOP** and a **CARDINAL** seated.

ARCHBISHOP
Knowing how near it touched the public morals,
And that our age is grown corrupt and rotten
By such excesses, we have sent to Rome,
Beseeching that his Holiness would aid
In curing the gross surfeit of the time,
By seasonable stop put here in Spain
To bull-fights and lewd dances on the stage.
All this you know.

CARDINAL
Know and approve.

ARCHBISHOP
And further,
That, by a mandate from his Holiness,
The first have been suppressed.

CARDINAL
I trust forever.
It was a cruel sport.

ARCHBISHOP
A barbarous pastime,
Disgraceful to the land that calls itself
Most Catholic and Christian.

CARDINAL
Yet the people
Murmur at this; and, if the public dances
Should be condemned upon too slight occasion,
Worse ills might follow than the ills we cure.
As Panem et Circenses was the cry
Among the Roman populace of old,
So Pan y Toros is the cry in Spain.
Hence I would act advisedly herein;

And therefore have induced your Grace to see
These national dances, ere we interdict them.

[Enter a **SERVANT**.

SERVANT
The dancing-girl, and with her the musicians
Your Grace was pleased to order, wait without.

ARCHBISHOP
Bid them come in. Now shall your eyes behold
In what angelic, yet voluptuous shape
The Devil came to tempt Saint Anthony.

[Enter **PRECIOSA**, with a mantle thrown over her head. She advances slowly, in modest, half-timid attitude.

CARDINAL [Aside]
O, what a fair and ministering angel
Was lost to heaven when this sweet woman fell!

PRECIOSA [Kneeling before the **ARCHBISHOP**]
I have obeyed the order of your Grace.
If I intrude upon your better hours,
I proffer this excuse, and here beseech
Your holy benediction.

ARCHBISHOP
May God bless thee,
And lead thee to a better life. Arise.

CARDINAL [Aside]
Her acts are modest, and her words discreet!
I did not look for this! Come hither, child.
Is thy name Preciosa?

PRECIOSA
Thus I am called.

CARDINAL
That is a Gypsy name. Who is thy father?

PRECIOSA
Beltran Cruzado, Count of the Cales.

ARCHBISHOP
I have a dim remembrance of that man:
He was a bold and reckless character,

A sun-burnt Ishmael!

CARDINAL
Dost thou remember
Thy earlier days?

PRECIOSA
Yes; by the Darro's side
My childhood passed. I can remember still
The river, and the mountains capped with snow
The village, where, yet a little child,
I told the traveller's fortune in the street;
The smuggler's horse, the brigand and the shepherd;
The march across the moor; the halt at noon;
The red fire of the evening camp, that lighted
The forest where we slept; and, further back,
As in a dream or in some former life,
Gardens and palace walls.

ARCHBISHOP
'T is the Alhambra,
Under whose towers the Gypsy camp was pitched.
But the time wears; and we would see thee dance.

PRECIOSA
Your Grace shall be obeyed.

[She lays aside her mantilla. The music of the cachucha is played, and the dance begins. The **ARCHBISHOP** and the **CARDINAL** look on with gravity and an occasional frown; then make signs to each other; and, as the dance continues, become more and more pleased and excited; and at length rise from their seats, throw their caps in the air, and applaud vehemently as the scene closes.

SCENE III. — The Prado. A Long Avenue of Trees Leading to the Gate of Atocha

On the right the dome and spires of a convent. A fountain. Evening, **DON CARLOS** and **HYPOLITO** meeting.

DON CARLOS
Hola! good evening, Don Hypolito.

HYPOLITO
And a good evening to my friend, Don Carlos.
Some lucky star has led my steps this way.
I was in search of you.

DON CATLOS

Command me always.

HYPOLITO
Do you remember, in Quevedo's Dreams,
The miser, who, upon the Day of Judgment,
Asks if his money-bags would rise?

DON CARLOS
I do;
But what of that?

HYPOLITO
I am that wretched man.

DON CARLOS
You mean to tell me yours have risen empty?

HYPOLITO
And amen! said my Cid the Campeador.

DON CARLOS
Pray, how much need you?

HYPOLITO
Some half-dozen ounces,
Which, with due interest—

DON CARLOS [Giving his purse]
What, am I a Jew
To put my moneys out at usury?
Here is my purse.

HYPOLITO
Thank you. A pretty purse.
Made by the hand of some fair Madrilena;
Perhaps a keepsake.

DON CARLOS
No, 't is at your service.

HYPOLITO
Thank you again. Lie there, good Chrysostom,
And with thy golden mouth remind me often,
I am the debtor of my friend.

DON CARLOS
But tell me,
Come you to-day from Alcala?

HYPOLITO
This moment.

DON CARLOS
And pray, how fares the brave Victorian?

HYPOLITO
Indifferent well; that is to say, not well.
A damsel has ensnared him with the glances
Of her dark, roving eyes, as herdsmen catch
A steer of Andalusia with a lazo.
He is in love.

DON CARLOS
And is it faring ill
To be in love?

HYPOLITO
In his case very ill.

DON CARLOS
Why so?

HYPOLITO
For many reasons. First and foremost,
Because he is in love with an ideal;
A creature of his own imagination;
A child of air; an echo of his heart;
And, like a lily on a river floating,
She floats upon the river of his thoughts!

DON CARLOS
A common thing with poets. But who is
This floating lily? For, in fine, some woman,
Some living woman,—not a mere ideal,—
Must wear the outward semblance of his thought.
Who is it? Tell me.

HYPOLITO
Well, it is a woman!
But, look you, from the coffer of his heart
He brings forth precious jewels to adorn her,
As pious priests adorn some favorite saint
With gems and gold, until at length she gleams
One blaze of glory. Without these, you know,
And the priest's benediction, 't is a doll.

DON CARLOS
Well, well! who is this doll?

HYPOLITO
Why, who do you think?

DON CARLOS
His cousin Violante.

HYPOLITO
Guess again.
To ease his laboring heart, in the last storm
He threw her overboard, with all her ingots.

DON CARLOS
I cannot guess; so tell me who it is.

HYPOLITO
Not I.

DON CARLOS
Why not?

HYPOLITO [Mysteriously]
Why? Because Mari Franca
Was married four leagues out of Salamanca!

DON CARLOS
Jesting aside, who is it?

HYPOLITO
Preciosa.

DON CARLOS
Impossible! The Count of Lara tells me
She is not virtuous.

HYPOLITO
Did I say she was?
The Roman Emperor Claudius had a wife
Whose name was Messalina, as I think;
Valeria Messalina was her name.
But hist! I see him yonder through the trees,
Walking as in a dream.

DON CARLOS
He comes this way.

HYPOLITO
It has been truly said by some wise man,
That money, grief, and love cannot be hidden.

[Enter **VICTORIAN** in front.

VICTORIAN
Where'er thy step has passed is holy ground!
These groves are sacred! I behold thee walking
Under these shadowy trees, where we have walked
At evening, and I feel thy presence now;
Feel that the place has taken a charm from thee,
And is forever hallowed.

HYPOLITO
Mark him well!
See how he strides away with lordly air,
Like that odd guest of stone, that grim Commander
Who comes to sup with Juan in the play.

DON CARLOS
What ho! Victorian!

HYPOLITO
Wilt thou sup with us?

VICTORIAN
Hola! amigos! Faith, I did not see you.
How fares Don Carlos?

DON CARLOS
At your service ever.

VICTORIAN
How is that young and green-eyed Gaditana
That you both wot of?

DON CARLOS
Ay, soft, emerald eyes!
She has gone back to Cadiz.

HYPOLITO
Ay de mi!

VICTORIAN
You are much to blame for letting her go back.
A pretty girl; and in her tender eyes
Just that soft shade of green we sometimes see

In evening skies.

HYPOLITO
But, speaking of green eyes,
Are thine green?

VICTORIAN
Not a whit. Why so?

HYPOLITO
I think
The slightest shade of green would be becoming,
For thou art jealous.

VICTORIAN
No, I am not jealous.

HYPOLITO
Thou shouldst be.

VICTORIAN
Why?

HYPOLITO
Because thou art in love.
And they who are in love are always jealous.
Therefore thou shouldst be.

VICTORIAN
Marry, is that all?
Farewell; I am in haste. Farewell, Don Carlos.
Thou sayest I should be jealous?

HYPOLITO
Ay, in truth
I fear there is reason. Be upon thy guard.
I hear it whispered that the Count of Lara
Lays siege to the same citadel.

VICTORIAN
Indeed!
Then he will have his labor for his pains.

HYPOLITO
He does not think so, and Don Carlos tells me
He boasts of his success.

VICTORIAN

How's this, Don Carlos?

DON CARLOS
Some hints of it I heard from his own lips.
He spoke but lightly of the lady's virtue,
As a gay man might speak.

VICTORIAN
Death and damnation!
I'll cut his lying tongue out of his mouth,
And throw it to my dog! But no, no, no!
This cannot be. You jest, indeed you jest.
Trifle with me no more. For otherwise
We are no longer friends. And so, fare well!

[Exit.

HYPOLITO
Now what a coil is here! The Avenging Child
Hunting the traitor Quadros to his death,
And the Moor Calaynos, when he rode
To Paris for the ears of Oliver,
Were nothing to him! O hot-headed youth!
But come; we will not follow. Let us join
The crowd that pours into the Prado. There
We shall find merrier company; I see
The Marialonzos and the Almavivas,
And fifty fans, that beckon me already.

[Exeunt.

SCENE IV. – Preciosa's Chamber

She is sitting, with a book in her hand, near a table, on which are flowers. A bird singing in its cage. The
COUNT of LARA enters behind unperceived.

PRECIOSA [Reads]
All are sleeping, weary heart!
Thou, thou only sleepless art!

Heigho! I wish Victorian were here.
I know not what it is makes me so restless!

[The bird sings.

Thou little prisoner with thy motley coat,

That from thy vaulted, wiry dungeon singest,
Like thee I am a captive, and, like thee,
I have a gentle jailer. Lack-a-day!

All are sleeping, weary heart!
Thou, thou only sleepless art!
All this throbbing, all this aching,
Evermore shall keep thee waking,
For a heart in sorrow breaking
Thinketh ever of its smart!

Thou speakest truly, poet! and methinks
More hearts are breaking in this world of ours
Than one would say. In distant villages
And solitudes remote, where winds have wafted
The barbed seeds of love, or birds of passage
Scattered them in their flight, do they take root,
And grow in silence, and in silence perish.
Who hears the falling of the forest leaf?
Or who takes note of every flower that dies?
Heigho! I wish Victorian would come.
Dolores!

[Turns to lay down her boot and perceives the **COUNT of LARA**.

Ha!

COUNT of LARA
Senora, pardon me.

PRECIOSA
How's this? Dolores!

COUNT of LARA
Pardon me—

PRECIOSA
Dolores!

COUNT of LARA
Be not alarmed; I found no one in waiting.
If I have been too bold—

PRECIOSA [Turning her back upon him]
You are too bold!
Retire! retire, and leave me!

COUNT of LARA

My dear lady,
First hear me! I beseech you, let me speak!
'T is for your good I come.

PRECIOSA [Turning toward him with indignation]
Begone! begone!
You are the Count of Lara, but your deeds
Would make the statues of your ancestors
Blush on their tombs! Is it Castilian honor,
Is it Castilian pride, to steal in here
Upon a friendless girl, to do her wrong?
O shame! shame! shame! that you, a nobleman,
Should be so little noble in your thoughts
As to send jewels here to win my love,
And think to buy my honor with your gold!
I have no words to tell you how I scorn you!
Begone! The sight of you is hateful to me!
Begone, I say!

COUNT of LARA
Be calm; I will not harm you.

PRECIOSA
Because you dare not.

COUNT of LARA
I dare anything!
Therefore beware! You are deceived in me.
In this false world, we do not always know
Who are our friends and who our enemies.
We all have enemies, and all need friends.
Even you, fair Preciosa, here at court
Have foes, who seek to wrong you.

PRECIOSA
If to this
I owe the honor of the present visit,
You might have spared the coming. Raving spoken,
Once more I beg you, leave me to myself.

COUNT of LARA
I thought it but a friendly part to tell you
What strange reports are current here in town.
For my own self, I do not credit them;
But there are many who, not knowing you,
Will lend a readier ear.

PRECIOSA

There was no need
That you should take upon yourself the duty
Of telling me these tales.

COUNT of LARA
Malicious tongues
Are ever busy with your name.

PRECIOSA
Alas!
I've no protectors. I am a poor girl,
Exposed to insults and unfeeling jests.
They wound me, yet I cannot shield myself.
I give no cause for these reports. I live
Retired; am visited by none.

COUNT of LARA
By none?
O, then, indeed, you are much wronged!

PRECIOSA
How mean you?

COUNT of LARA
Nay, nay; I will not wound your gentle soul
By the report of idle tales.

PRECIOSA
Speak out!
What are these idle tales? You need not spare me.

COUNT of LARA
I will deal frankly with you. Pardon me
This window, as I think, looks toward the street,
And this into the Prado, does it not?
In yon high house, beyond the garden wall,—
You see the roof there just above the trees,—
There lives a friend, who told me yesterday,
That on a certain night,—be not offended
If I too plainly speak,—he saw a man
Climb to your chamber window. You are silent!
I would not blame you, being young and fair—

[He tries to embrace her. She starts back, and draws a dagger from her bosom.

PRECIOSA
Beware! beware! I am a Gypsy girl!
Lay not your hand upon me. One step nearer

And I will strike!

COUNT of LARA
Pray you, put up that dagger.
Fear not.

PRECIOSA
I do not fear. I have a heart
In whose strength I can trust.

COUNT of LARA
Listen to me
I come here as your friend,—I am your friend,—
And by a single word can put a stop
To all those idle tales, and make your name
Spotless as lilies are. Here on my knees,
Fair Preciosa! on my knees I swear,
I love you even to madness, and that love
Has driven me to break the rules of custom,
And force myself unasked into your presence.

[**VICTORIAN** enters behind.

PRECIOSA
Rise, Count of Lara! That is not the place
For such as you are. It becomes you not
To kneel before me. I am strangely moved
To see one of your rank thus low and humbled;
For your sake I will put aside all anger,
All unkind feeling, all dislike, and speak
In gentleness, as most becomes a woman,
And as my heart now prompts me. I no more
Will hate you, for all hate is painful to me.
But if, without offending modesty
And that reserve which is a woman's glory,
I may speak freely, I will teach my heart
To love you.

COUNT of LARA
O sweet angel!

PRECIOSA
Ay, in truth,
Far better than you love yourself or me.

COUNT of LARA
Give me some sign of this,—the slightest token.
Let me but kiss your hand!

PRECIOSA

Nay, come no nearer.
The words I utter are its sign and token.
Misunderstand me not! Be not deceived!
The love wherewith I love you is not such
As you would offer me. For you come here
To take from me the only thing I have,
My honor. You are wealthy, you have friends
And kindred, and a thousand pleasant hopes
That fill your heart with happiness; but I
Am poor, and friendless, having but one treasure,
And you would take that from me, and for what?
To flatter your own vanity, and make me
What you would most despise. O sir, such love,
That seeks to harm me, cannot be true love.
Indeed it cannot. But my love for you
Is of a different kind. It seeks your good.
It is a holier feeling. It rebukes
Your earthly passion, your unchaste desires,
And bids you look into your heart, and see
How you do wrong that better nature in you,
And grieve your soul with sin.

COUNT of LARA

I swear to you,
I would not harm you; I would only love you.
I would not take your honor, but restore it,
And in return I ask but some slight mark
Of your affection. If indeed you love me,
As you confess you do, O let me thus
With this embrace—

VICTORIAN [Rushing forward]

Hold! hold! This is too much.
What means this outrage?

COUNT of LARA

First, what right have you
To question thus a nobleman of Spain?

VICTORIAN

I too am noble, and you are no more!
Out of my sight!

COUNT of LARA

Are you the master here?

VICTORIAN
Ay, here and elsewhere, when the wrong of others
Gives me the right!

PRECIOSA [To **COUNT of LARA**]
Go! I beseech you, go!

VICTORIAN
I shall have business with you, Count, anon!

COUNT of LARA
You cannot come too soon!

[Exit.

PRECIOSA
Victorian!
O, we have been betrayed!

VICTORIAN
Ha! ha! betrayed!
'T is I have been betrayed, not we!—not we!

PRECIOSA
Dost thou imagine—

VICTORIAN
I imagine nothing;
I see how 't is thou whilest the time away
When I am gone!

PRECIOSA
O speak not in that tone!
It wounds me deeply.

VICTORIAN
'T was not meant to flatter.

PRECIOSA
Too well thou knowest the presence of that man
Is hateful to me!

VICTORIAN
Yet I saw thee stand
And listen to him, when he told his love.

PRECIOSA
I did not heed his words.

VICTORIAN
Indeed thou didst,
And answeredst them with love.

PRECIOSA
Hadst thou heard all—

VICTORIAN
I heard enough.

PRECIOSA
Be not so angry with me.

VICTORIAN
I am not angry; I am very calm.

PRECIOSA
If thou wilt let me speak—

VICTORIAN
Nay, say no more.
I know too much already. Thou art false!
I do not like these Gypsy marriages!
Where is the ring I gave thee?

PRECIOSA
In my casket.

VICTORIAN
There let it rest! I would not have thee wear it:
I thought thee spotless, and thou art polluted!

PRECIOSA
I call the Heavens to witness—

VICTORIAN
Nay, nay, nay!
Take not the name of Heaven upon thy lips!
They are forsworn!

PRECIOSA
Victorian! dear Victorian!

VICTORIAN
I gave up all for thee; myself, my fame,
My hopes of fortune, ay, my very soul!
And thou hast been my ruin! Now, go on!

Laugh at my folly with thy paramour,
And, sitting on the Count of Lara's knee,
Say what a poor, fond fool Victorian was!

[He casts her from him and rushes out.

PRECIOSA
And this from thee!

[Scene closes.

SCENE V. — The Count of Lara's Rooms

Enter the **COUNT of LARA**.

COUNT of LARA
There's nothing in this world so sweet as love,
And next to love the sweetest thing is hate!
I've learned to hate, and therefore am revenged.
A silly girl to play the prude with me!
The fire that I have kindled—

[Enter **FRANCISCO**.

Well, Francisco,
What tidings from Don Juan?

FRANCISCO
Good, my lord;
He will be present.

COUNT of LARA
And the Duke of Lermos?

FRANCISCO
Was not at home.

COUNT of LARA
How with the rest?

FRANCISCO
I've found
The men you wanted. They will all be there,
And at the given signal raise a whirlwind
Of such discordant noises, that the dance
Must cease for lack of music.

COUNT of LARA

Bravely done.
Ah! little dost thou dream, sweet Preciosa,
What lies in wait for thee. Sleep shall not close
Thine eyes this night! Give me my cloak and sword.

[Exeunt.

SCENE VI. — A Retired Spot Beyond the City Gates

Enter **VICTORIAN** and **HYPOLITO**.

VICTORIAN

O shame! O shame! Why do I walk abroad
By daylight, when the very sunshine mocks me,
And voices, and familiar sights and sounds
Cry, "Hide thyself!" O what a thin partition
Doth shut out from the curious world the knowledge
Of evil deeds that have been done in darkness!
Disgrace has many tongues. My fears are windows,
Through which all eyes seem gazing. Every face
Expresses some suspicion of my shame,
And in derision seems to smile at me!

HYPOLITO

Did I not caution thee? Did I not tell thee
I was but half persuaded of her virtue?

VICTORIAN

And yet, Hypolito, we may be wrong,
We may be over-hasty in condemning!
The Count of Lara is a cursed villain.

HYPOLITO

And therefore is she cursed, loving him.

VICTORIAN

She does not love him! 'T is for gold! for gold!

HYPOLITO

Ay, but remember, in the public streets
He shows a golden ring the Gypsy gave him,
A serpent with a ruby in its mouth.

VICTORIAN

She had that ring from me! God! she is false!
But I will be revenged! The hour is passed.
Where stays the coward?

HYPOLITO
Nay, he is no coward;
A villain, if thou wilt, but not a coward.
I've seen him play with swords; it is his pastime.
And therefore be not over-confident,
He'll task thy skill anon. Look, here he comes.

[Enter **COUNT of LARA** followed by **FRANCISCO.**

COUNT of LARA
Good evening, gentlemen.

HYPOLITO
Good evening, Count.

COUNT of LARA
I trust I have not kept you long in waiting.

VICTORIAN
Not long, and yet too long. Are you prepared?

COUNT of LARA
I am.

HYPOLITO
It grieves me much to see this quarrel
Between you, gentlemen. Is there no way
Left open to accord this difference,
But you must make one with your swords?

VICTORIAN
No! none!
I do entreat thee, dear Hypolito,
Stand not between me an my foe. Too long
Our tongues have spoken. Let these tongues of steel
End our debate. Upon your guard, Sir Count.

[They fight. **VICTORIAN** disarms the **COUNT of LARA.**

Your life is mine; and what shall now withhold me
From sending your vile soul to its account?

COUNT of LARA
Strike! strike!

VICTORIAN
You are disarmed. I will not kill you.
I will not murder you. Take up your sword.

[**FRANCISCO** hands the **COUNT of LARA** his sword, and **HYPOLITO** interposes.

HYPOLITO
Enough! Let it end here! The Count of Lara
Has shown himself a brave man, and Victorian
A generous one, as ever. Now be friends.
Put up your swords; for, to speak frankly to you,
Your cause of quarrel is too slight a thing
To move you to extremes.

COUNT of LARA
I am content,
I sought no quarrel. A few hasty words,
Spoken in the heat of blood, have led to this.

VICTORIAN
Nay, something more than that.

COUNT of LARA
I understand you.
Therein I did not mean to cross your path.
To me the door stood open, as to others.
But, had I known the girl belonged to you,
Never would I have sought to win her from you.
The truth stands now revealed; she has been false
To both of us.

VICTORIAN
Ay, false as hell itself!

COUNT of LARA
In truth, I did not seek her; she sought me;
And told me how to win her, telling me
The hours when she was oftenest left alone.

VICTORIAN
Say, can you prove this to me? O, pluck out
These awful doubts, that goad me into madness!
Let me know all! all! all!

COUNT of LARA
You shall know all.
Here is my page, who was the messenger

Between us. Question him. Was it not so,
Francisco?

FRANCISCO
Ay, my lord.

COUNT of LARA
If further proof
Is needful, I have here a ring she gave me.

VICTORIAN
Pray let me see that ring! It is the same!

[Throws it upon the ground, and tramples upon it.

Thus may she perish who once wore that ring!
Thus do I spurn her from me; do thus trample
Her memory in the dust! O Count of Lara,
We both have been abused, been much abused!
I thank you for your courtesy and frankness.
Though, like the surgeon's hand, yours gave me pain,
Yet it has cured my blindness, and I thank you.
I now can see the folly I have done,
Though 't is, alas! too late. So fare you well!
To-night I leave this hateful town forever.
Regard me as your friend. Once more farewell!

HYPOLITO
Farewell, Sir Count.

[Exeunt **VICTORIAN** and **HYPOLITO**.

COUNT of LARA
Farewell! farewell! farewell!
Thus have I cleared the field of my worst foe!
I have none else to fear; the fight is done,
The citadel is stormed, the victory won!

[Exit with **FRANCISCO**.

SCENE VII. — A Lane in the Suburbs. Night

Enter **CRUZADO** and **BARTOLOME**.

CRUZADO
And so, Bartolome, the expedition failed. But where wast thou for the most part?

BARTOLOME

In the Guadarrama mountains, near San Ildefonso.

CRUZADO

And thou bringest nothing back with thee? Didst thou rob no one?

BARTOLOME

There was no one to rob, save a party of students from Segovia, who looked as if they would rob us; and a jolly little friar, who had nothing in his pockets but a missal and a loaf of bread.

CRUZADO

Pray, then, what brings thee back to Madrid?

BARTOLOME

First tell me what keeps thee here?

CRUZADO

Preciosa.

BARTOLOME

And she brings me back. Hast thou forgotten thy promise?

CRUZADO

The two years are not passed yet. Wait patiently. The girl shall be thine.

BARTOLOME

I hear she has a Busne lover.

CRUZADO

That is nothing.

BARTOLOME

I do not like it. I hate him,—the son of a Busne harlot. He goes in and out, and speaks with her alone, and I must stand aside, and wait his pleasure.

CRUZADO

Be patient, I say. Thou shalt have thy revenge. When the time comes, thou shalt waylay him.

BARTOLOME

Meanwhile, show me her house.

CRUZADO

Come this way. But thou wilt not find her. She dances at the play to-night.

BARTOLOME

No matter. Show me the house.

[Exeunt.

SCENE VIII. — The Theatre

The orchestra plays the cachucha. Sound of castanets behind the scenes. The curtain rises, and discovers **PRECIOSA** in the attitude of commencing the dance. The cachucha. Tumult; hisses; cries of "Brava!" and "Afuera!" She falters and pauses. The music stops. General confusion. **PRECIOSA** faints.

SCENE IX. — The Count OF Lara's Chambers

The **COUNT of LARA** and his **FRIENDS** at supper.

COUNT of LARA
So, Caballeros, once more many thanks!
You have stood by me bravely in this matter.
Pray fill your glasses.

DON JUAN
Did you mark, Don Luis,
How pale she looked, when first the noise began,
And then stood still, with her large eyes dilated!
Her nostrils spread! her lips apart! Her bosom
Tumultuous as the sea!

DON LUIS
I pitied her.

COUNT of LARA
Her pride is humbled; and this very night
I mean to visit her.

DON JUAN
Will you serenade her?

COUNT of LARA
No music! no more music!

DON LUIS
Why not music?
It softens many hearts.

COUNT of LARA
Not in the humor
She now is in. Music would madden her.

DON JUAN
Try golden cymbals.

DON LUIS
Yes, try Don Dinero;
A mighty wooer is your Don Dinero.

COUNT of LARA
To tell the truth, then, I have bribed her maid.
But, Caballeros, you dislike this wine.
A bumper and away; for the night wears.
A health to Preciosa.

[They rise and drink.

ALL
Preciosa.

COUNT of LARA [Holding up his glass]
Thou bright and flaming minister of Love!
Thou wonderful magician! who hast stolen
My secret from me, and mid sighs of passion
Caught from my lips, with red and fiery tongue,
Her precious name! O nevermore henceforth
Shall mortal lips press thine; and nevermore
A mortal name be whispered in thine ear.
Go! keep my secret!

[Drinks and dashes the goblet down.

DON JUAN
Ite! missa est!

[Scene closes.

SCENE X. — Street and Garden Wall. Night.

Enter **CRUZADO** and **BARTOLOME**.

CRUZADO
This is the garden wall, and above it, yonder, is her house. The window in which thou seest the light is her window. But we will not go in now.

BARTOLOME
Why not?

CRUZADO
Because she is not at home.

BARTOLOME
No matter; we can wait. But how is this? The gate is bolted.

[Sound of guitars and **VOICES** in a neighboring street.

Hark! There comes her lover with his infernal serenade! Hark!

SONG.

Good night! Good night, beloved!
I come to watch o'er thee!
To be near thee,—to be near thee,
Alone is peace for me.

Thine eyes are stars of morning,
Thy lips are crimson flowers!
Good night! Good night beloved,
While I count the weary hours.

CRUZADO
They are not coming this way.

BARTOLOME
Wait, they begin again.

SONG [Coming nearer].

Ah! thou moon that shinest
Argent-clear above!
All night long enlighten
My sweet lady-love!
Moon that shinest,
All night long enlighten!

BARTOLOME
Woe be to him, if he comes this way!

CRUZADO
Be quiet, they are passing down the street.

SONG [Dying away]

The nuns in the cloister
Sang to each other;

For so many sisters
Is there not one brother!
Ay, for the partridge, mother!
The cat has run away with the partridge!
Puss! puss! puss!

BARTOLOME
Follow that! follow that!
Come with me. Puss! puss!

[Exeunt. On the opposite side enter the **COUNT of LARA** and **GENTLEMEN**, with **FRANCISCO**.

COUNT of LARA
The gate is fast. Over the wall, Francisco,
And draw the bolt. There, so, and so, and over.
Now, gentlemen, come in, and help me scale
Yon balcony. How now? Her light still burns.
Move warily. Make fast the gate, Francisco.

[Exeunt. Re-enter **CRUZADO** and **BARTOLOME**.

BARTOLOME
They went in at the gate. Hark! I hear them in the garden.

[Tries the gate.

Bolted again! Vive Cristo! Follow me over the wall.

[They climb the wall.

SCENE XI. – Preciosa's Bedchamber. Midnight.

She is sleeping in an armchair, in an undress. **DOLORES** watching her.

DOLORES
She sleeps at last!

[Opens the window, and listens.

All silent in the street,
And in the garden. Hark!

PRECIOSA [In her sleep]
I must go hence!
Give me my cloak!

DOLORES
He comes! I hear his footsteps.

PRECIOSA
Go tell them that I cannot dance to-night;
I am too ill! Look at me! See the fever
That burns upon my cheek! I must go hence.
I am too weak to dance.

[Signal from the garden.

DOLORES [From the window]
Who's there?

VOICE [From below]
A friend.

DOLORES
I will undo the door. Wait till I come.

PRECIOSA
I must go hence. I pray you do not harm me!
Shame! shame! to treat a feeble woman thus!
Be you but kind, I will do all things for you.
I'm ready now,—give me my castanets.
Where is Victorian? Oh, those hateful lamps!
They glare upon me like an evil eye.
I cannot stay. Hark! how they mock at me!
They hiss at me like serpents! Save me! save me!

[She wakes.

How late is it, Dolores?

DOLORES
It is midnight.

PRECIOSA
We must be patient. Smooth this pillow for me.

[She sleeps again. Noise from the garden, and **VOICES**.

VOICE
Muera!

ANOTHER VOICE
O villains! villains!

COUNT of LARA
So! have at you!

VOICE
Take that!

COUNT of LARA
O, I am wounded!

DOLORES [Shutting the window]
Jesu Maria!

SCENE I. — A Cross-Road Through a Wood

In the background a distant village spire. **VICTORIAN** and **HYPOLITO**, as travelling students, with guitars, sitting under the trees. **HYPOLITO** plays and sings.

SONG.

Ah, Love!
Perjured, false, treacherous Love!
Enemy
Of all that mankind may not rue!
Most untrue
To him who keeps most faith with thee.
Woe is me!
The falcon has the eyes of the dove.
Ah, Love!
Perjured, false, treacherous Love!

VICTORIAN
Yes, Love is ever busy with his shuttle,
Is ever weaving into life's dull warp
Bright, gorgeous flowers and scenes Arcadian;
Hanging our gloomy prison-house about
With tapestries, that make its walls dilate
In never-ending vistas of delight.

HYPOLITO
Thinking to walk in those Arcadian pastures,
Thou hast run thy noble head against the wall.

SONG [Continued]

Thy deceits
Give us clearly to comprehend,
Whither tend
All thy pleasures, all thy sweets!
They are cheats,
Thorns below and flowers above.
Ah, Love!
Perjured, false, treacherous Love!

VICTORIAN
A very pretty song. I thank thee for it.

HYPOLITO
It suits thy case.

VICTORIAN
Indeed, I think it does.
What wise man wrote it?

HYPOLITO
Lopez Maldonado.

VICTORIAN
In truth, a pretty song.

HYPOLITO
With much truth in it.
I hope thou wilt profit by it; and in earnest
Try to forget this lady of thy love.

VICTORIAN
I will forget her! All dear recollections
Pressed in my heart, like flowers within a book,
Shall be torn out, and scattered to the winds!
I will forget her! But perhaps hereafter,
When she shall learn how heartless is the world,
A voice within her will repeat my name,
And she will say, "He was indeed my friend!"
O, would I were a soldier, not a scholar,
That the loud march, the deafening beat of drums,
The shattering blast of the brass-throated trumpet,
The din of arms, the onslaught and the storm,
And a swift death, might make me deaf forever
To the upbraidings of this foolish heart!

HYPOLITO
Then let that foolish heart upbraid no more!
To conquer love, one need but will to conquer.

VICTORIAN

Yet, good Hypolito, it is in vain
I throw into Oblivion's sea the sword
That pierces me; for, like Excalibar,
With gemmed and flashing hilt, it will not sink.
There rises from below a hand that grasp it,
And waves it in the air; and wailing voices
Are heard along the shore.

HYPOLITO

And yet at last
Down sank Excalibar to rise no more.
This is not well. In truth, it vexes me.
Instead of whistling to the steeds of Time,
To make them jog on merrily with life's burden,
Like a dead weight thou hangest on the wheels.
Thou art too young, too full of lusty health
To talk of dying.

VICTORIAN

Yet I fain would die!
To go through life, unloving and unloved;
To feel that thirst and hunger of the soul
We cannot still; that longing, that wild impulse,
And struggle after something we have not
And cannot have; the effort to be strong
And, like the Spartan boy, to smile, and smile,
While secret wounds do bleed beneath our cloaks
All this the dead feel not,—the dead alone!
Would I were with them!

HYPOLITO

We shall all be soon.

VICTORIAN

It cannot be too soon; for I am weary
Of the bewildering masquerade of Life,
Where strangers walk as friends, and friends as strangers;
Where whispers overheard betray false hearts;
And through the mazes of the crowd we chase
Some form of loveliness, that smiles, and beckons,
And cheats us with fair words, only to leave us
A mockery and a jest; maddened,—confused,—
Not knowing friend from foe.

HYPOLITO

Why seek to know?

Enjoy the merry shrove-tide of thy youth!
Take each fair mask for what it gives itself,
Nor strive to look beneath it.

VICTORIAN
I confess,
That were the wiser part. But Hope no longer
Comforts my soul. I am a wretched man,
Much like a poor and shipwrecked mariner,
Who, struggling to climb up into the boat,
Has both his bruised and bleeding hands cut off,
And sinks again into the weltering sea,
Helpless and hopeless!

HYPOLITO
Yet thou shalt not perish.
The strength of thine own arm is thy salvation.
Above thy head, through rifted clouds, there shines
A glorious star. Be patient. Trust thy star!

[Sound of a village belt in the distance.

VICTORIAN
Ave Maria! I hear the sacristan
Ringing the chimes from yonder village belfry!
A solemn sound, that echoes far and wide
Over the red roofs of the cottages,
And bids the laboring hind a-field, the shepherd,
Guarding his flock, the lonely muleteer,
And all the crowd in village streets, stand still,
And breathe a prayer unto the blessed Virgin!

HYPOLITO
Amen! amen! Not half a league from hence
The village lies.

VICTORIAN
This path will lead us to it,
Over the wheat-fields, where the shadows sail
Across the running sea, now green, now blue,
And, like an idle mariner on the main,
Whistles the quail. Come, let us hasten on.

[Exeunt.

SCENE II. — Public Square in the Village of Guadarrama

The Ave Maria still tolling. A **CROWD** of villagers, with their hats in their hands, as if in prayer. In front, a group of **GYPSIES**. The bell rings a merrier peal. A Gypsy dance. Enter **PANCHO**, followed by **PEDRO CRESPO**.

PANCHO
Make room, ye vagabonds and Gypsy thieves!
Make room for the Alcalde and for me!

PEDRO CRESPO
Keep silence all! I have an edict here
From our most gracious lord, the King of Spain,
Jerusalem, and the Canary Islands,
Which I shall publish in the market-place.
Open your ears and listen!

[Enter the **PADRE CURA** at the door of his cottage.

PADRE CURA
Good day! and, pray you, hear this edict read.

PADRE CURA
Good day, and God be with you! Pray, what is it?

PEDRO CRESPO
An act of banishment against the Gypsies!

[Agitation and murmurs in the crowd.

PANCHO
Silence!

PEDRO CRESPO [Reads].
"I hereby order and command,
That the Egyptian an Chaldean strangers,
Known by the name of Gypsies, shall henceforth
Be banished from the realm, as vagabonds
And beggars; and if, after seventy days,
Any be found within our kingdom's bounds,
They shall receive a hundred lashes each;
The second time, shall have their ears cut off;
The third, be slaves for life to him who takes them,
Or burnt as heretics. Signed, I, the King."
Vile miscreants and creatures unbaptized!
You hear the law! Obey and disappear!

PANCHO
And if in seventy days you are not gone,

Dead or alive I make you all my slaves.

[The **GYPSIES** go out in confusion, showing signs of fear and discontent. **PANCHO** follows.

PADRE CURA
A righteous law! A very righteous law!
Pray you, sit down.

PEDRO CRESPO
I thank you heartily.

[They seat themselves on a bench at the Padre Cura's door. Sound of guitars heard at a distance, approaching during the dialogue which follows.

A very righteous judgment, as you say.
Now tell me, Padre Cura,—you know all things,
How came these Gypsies into Spain?

PADRE CURA
Why, look you;
They came with Hercules from Palestine,
And hence are thieves and vagrants, Sir Alcalde,
As the Simoniacs from Simon Magus,
And, look you, as Fray Jayme Bleda says,
There are a hundred marks to prove a Moor
Is not a Christian, so 't is with the Gypsies.
They never marry, never go to mass,
Never baptize their children, nor keep Lent,
Nor see the inside of a church,—nor—nor—

PEDRO CRESPO
Good reasons, good, substantial reasons all!
No matter for the other ninety-five.
They should be burnt, I see it plain enough,
They should be bunt.

[Enter **VICTORIAN** and **HYPOLITO** playing.

PADRE CURA
And pray, whom have we here?

PEDRO CRESPO
More vagrants! By Saint Lazarus, more vagrants!

HYPOLITO
Good evening, gentlemen! Is this Guadarrama?

PADRE CURA

Yes, Guadarrama, and good evening to you.

HYPOLITO
We seek the Padre Cura of the village;
And, judging from your dress and reverend mien,
You must be he.

PADRE CURA
I am. Pray, what's your pleasure?

HYPOLITO
We are poor students, traveling in vacation.
You know this mark?

[Touching the wooden spoon in his hat-band.

PADRE CURA [Joyfully]
Ay, know it, and have worn it.

PEDRO CRESPO [Aside]
Soup-eaters! by the mass! The worst of vagrants!
And there's no law against them. Sir, your servant.

[Exit.

PADRE CURA
Your servant, Pedro Crespo.

HYPOLITO
Padre Cura,
Front the first moment I beheld your face,
I said within myself, "This is the man!"
There is a certain something in your looks,
A certain scholar-like and studious something,—
You understand,—which cannot be mistaken;
Which marks you as a very learned man,
In fine, as one of us.

VICTORIAN [Aside]
What impudence!

HYPOLITO
As we approached, I said to my companion,
"That is the Padre Cura; mark my words!"
Meaning your Grace. "The other man," said I,
Who sits so awkwardly upon the bench,
Must be the sacristan."

PADRE CURA

Ah! said you so?
Why, that was Pedro Crespo, the alcalde!

HYPOLITO

Indeed! you much astonish me! His air
Was not so full of dignity and grace
As an alcalde's should be.

PADRE CURA

That is true.
He's out of humor with some vagrant Gypsies,
Who have their camp here in the neighborhood.
There's nothing so undignified as anger.

HYPOLITO

The Padre Cura will excuse our boldness,
If, from his well-known hospitality,
We crave a lodging for the night.

PADRE CURA

I pray you!
You do me honor! I am but too happy
To have such guests beneath my humble roof.
It is not often that I have occasion
To speak with scholars; and Emollit mores,
Nec sinit esse feros, Cicero says.

HYPOLITO

'T is Ovid, is it not?

PADRE CURA

No, Cicero.

HYPOLITO

Your Grace is right. You are the better scholar.
Now what a dunce was I to think it Ovid!
But hang me if it is not! [Aside.]

PADRE CURA

Pass this way.
He was a very great man, was Cicero!
Pray you, go in, go in! no ceremony.

[Exeunt.

Enter the **PADRE CURA** and **HYPOLITO**.

PADRE CURA
So then, Senor, you come from Alcala.
I am glad to hear it. It was there I studied.

HYPOLITO
And left behind an honored name, no doubt.
How may I call your Grace?

PADRE CURA
Geronimo
De Santillana, at your Honor's service.

HYPOLITO
Descended from the Marquis Santillana?
From the distinguished poet?

PADRE CURA
From the Marquis,
Not from the poet.

HYPOLITO
Why, they were the same.
Let me embrace you! O some lucky star
Has brought me hither! Yet once more!—once more!
Your name is ever green in Alcala,
And our professor, when we are unruly,
Will shake his hoary head, and say, "Alas!
It was not so in Santillana's time!"

PADRE CURA
I did not think my name remembered there.

HYPOLITO
More than remembered; it is idolized.

PADRE CURA
Of what professor speak you?

HYPOLITO
Timoneda.

PADRE CURA
I don't remember any Timoneda.

HYPOLITO
A grave and sombre man, whose beetling brow
O'erhangs the rushing current of his speech
As rocks o'er rivers hang. Have you forgotten?

PADRE CURA
Indeed, I have. O, those were pleasant days,
Those college days! I ne'er shall see the like!
I had not buried then so many hopes!
I had not buried then so many friends!
I've turned my back on what was then before me;
And the bright faces of my young companions
Are wrinkled like my own, or are no more.
Do you remember Cueva?

HYPOLITO
Cueva? Cueva?

PADRE CURA
Fool that I am! He was before your time.
You're a mere boy, and I am an old man.

HYPOLITO
I should not like to try my strength with you.

PADRE CURA
Well, well. But I forget; you must be hungry.
Martina! ho! Martina! 'T is my niece.

[Enter **MARTINA**.

HYPOLITO
You may be proud of such a niece as that.
I wish I had a niece. Emollit mores.
[Aside.]
He was a very great man, was Cicero!
Your servant, fair Martina.

MARTINA
Servant, sir.

PADRE CURA
This gentleman is hungry. See thou to it.
Let us have supper.

MARTINA
'T will be ready soon.

PADRE CURA
And bring a bottle of my Val-de-Penas
Out of the cellar. Stay; I'll go myself.
Pray you. Senor, excuse me.

[Exit.

HYPOLITO
Hist! Martina!
One word with you. Bless me I what handsome eyes!
To-day there have been Gypsies in the village.
Is it not so?

MARTINA
There have been Gypsies here.

HYPOLITO
Yes, and have told your fortune.

MARTINA [Embarrassed]
Told my fortune?

HYPOLITO
Yes, yes; I know they did. Give me your hand.
I'll tell you what they said. They said,—they said,
The shepherd boy that loved you was a clown,
And him you should not marry. Was it not?

MARTINA [Surprised]
How know you that?

HYPOLITO
O, I know more than that,
What a soft, little hand! And then they said,
A cavalier from court, handsome, and tall
And rich, should come one day to marry you,
And you should be a lady. Was it not!
He has arrived, the handsome cavalier.

[Tries to kiss her. She runs off. Enter **VICTORIAN**, with a letter.

VICTORIAN
The muleteer has come.

HYPOLITO
So soon?

VICTORIAN

I found him
Sitting at supper by the tavern door,
And, from a pitcher that he held aloft
His whole arm's length, drinking the blood-red wine.

HYPOLITO
What news from Court?

VICTORIAN
He brought this letter only.

[Reads.]
O cursed perfidy! Why did I let
That lying tongue deceive me! Preciosa,
Sweet Preciosa! how art thou avenged!

HYPOLITO
What news is this, that makes thy cheek turn pale,
And thy hand tremble?

VICTORIAN
O, most infamous!
The Count of Lara is a worthless villain!

HYPOLITO
That is no news, forsooth.

VICTORIAN
He strove in vain
To steal from me the jewel of my soul,
The love of Preciosa. Not succeeding,
He swore to be revenged; and set on foot
A plot to ruin her, which has succeeded.
She has been hissed and hooted from the stage,
Her reputation stained by slanderous lies
Too foul to speak of; and, once more a beggar,
She roams a wanderer over God's green earth
Housing with Gypsies!

HYPOLITO
To renew again
The Age of Gold, and make the shepherd swains
Desperate with love, like Gasper Gil's Diana.
Redit et Virgo!

VICTORIAN
Dear Hypolito,
How have I wronged that meek, confiding heart!

I will go seek for her; and with my tears
Wash out the wrong I've done her!

HYPOLITO
O beware!
Act not that folly o'er again.

VICTORIAN
Ay, folly,
Delusion, madness, call it what thou wilt,
I will confess my weakness,—I still love her!
Still fondly love her!

[Enter the **PADRE CURA**.

HYPOLITO
Tell us, Padre Cura,
Who are these Gypsies in the neighborhood?

PADRE CURA
Beltran Cruzado and his crew.

VICTORIAN
Kind Heaven,
I thank thee! She is found! is found again!

HYPOLITO
And have they with them a pale, beautiful girl,
Called Preciosa?

PADRE CURA
Ay, a pretty girl.
The gentleman seems moved.

HYPOLITO
Yes, moved with hunger,
He is half famished with this long day's journey.

PADRE CURA
Then, pray you, come this way. The supper waits.

[Exeunt.

SCENE IV. — A Post-House on the Road to Segovia, Not Far from the Village of Guadarrama

Enter **CHISPA**, cracking a whip, and singing the cachucha.

CHISPA

Halloo! Don Fulano! Let us have horses, and quickly. Alas, poor Chispa! what a dog's life dost thou lead! I thought, when I left my old master Victorian, the student, to serve my new master Don Carlos, the gentleman, that I, too, should lead the life of a gentleman; should go to bed early, and get up late. For when the abbot plays cards, what can you expect of the friars? But, in running away from the thunder, I have run into the lightning. Here I am in hot chase after my master and his Gypsy girl. And a good beginning of the week it is, as he said who was hanged on Monday morning.

[Enter **DON CARLOS**.

DON CARLOS

Are not the horses ready yet?

CHISPA

I should think not, for the hostler seems to be asleep. Ho! within there! Horses! horses! horses!

[He knocks at the gate with his whip, and enter **MOSQUITO**, putting on his jacket.

MOSQUITO

Pray, have a little patience. I'm not a musket.

CHISPA

Health and pistareens! I'm glad to see you come on dancing, padre! Pray, what's the news?

MOSQUITO

You cannot have fresh horses; because there are none.

CHISPA

Cachiporra! Throw that bone to another dog. Do I look like your aunt?

MOSQUITO

No; she has a beard.

CHISPA

Go to! go to!

MOSQUITO

Are you from Madrid?

CHISPA

Yes; and going to Estramadura. Get us horses.

MOSQUITO

What's the news at Court?

CHISPA

Why, the latest news is, that I am going to set up a coach, and I have already bought the whip.

[Strikes him round the legs.

MOSQUITO
Oh! oh! You hurt me!

DON CARLOS
Enough of this folly. Let us have horses.

[Gives money to **MOSQUITO**.

It is almost dark; and we are in haste. But tell me, has a band of Gypsies passed this way of late?

MOSQUITO
Yes; and they are still in the neighborhood.

DON CARLOS
And where?

MOSQUITO
Across the fields yonder, in the woods near Guadarrama.

[Exit.

DON CARLOS
Now this is lucky. We will visit the Gypsy camp.

CHISPA
Are you not afraid of the evil eye? Have you a stag's horn with you?

DON CARLOS
Fear not. We will pass the night at the village.

CHISPA
And sleep like the Squires of Hernan Daza, nine under one blanket.

DON CARLOS
I hope we may find the Preciosa among them.

CHISPA
Among the Squires?

DON CARLOS
No; among the Gypsies, blockhead!

CHISPA
I hope we may; for we are giving ourselves trouble enough on her account. Don't you think so?
However, there is no catching trout without wetting one's trousers. Yonder come the horses.

[Exeunt.

SCENE V. — The Gypsy Camp in the Forest. Night.

GYPSIES working at a forge. Others playing cards by the firelight. **GYPSIES** [At the forge sing]

On the top of a mountain I stand,
With a crown of red gold in my hand,
Wild Moors come trooping over the lea
O how from their fury shall I flee, flee, flee?
O how from their fury shall I flee?

FIRST GYPSY [Playing]
Down with your John-Dorados, my pigeon.
Down with your John-Dorados, and let us make an end.

GYPSIES [At the forge sing]

Loud sang the Spanish cavalier,
And thus his ditty ran;
God send the Gypsy lassie here,
And not the Gypsy man.

FIRST GYPSY [Playing]
There you are in your morocco!

SECOND GYPSY
One more game. The Alcalde's doves against the
Padre Cura's new moon.

FIRST GYPSY
Have at you, Chirelin.

GYPSIES [At the forge sing]

At midnight, when the moon began
To show her silver flame,
There came to him no Gypsy man,
The Gypsy lassie came.

[Enter **BELTRAN CRUZADO**.

CRUZADO
Come hither, Murcigalleros and Rastilleros; leave work, leave play; listen to your orders for the night.
[Speaking to the right.] You will get you to the village, mark you, by the stone cross.

GYPSIES
Ay!

CRUZADO [To the left]
And you, by the pole with the hermit's head upon it.

GYPSIES
Ay!

CRUZADO
As soon as you see the planets are out, in with you, and
be busy with the ten commandments, under the sly, and Saint
Martin asleep. D'ye hear?

GYPSIES
Ay!

CRUZADO
Keep your lanterns open, and, if you see a goblin or a papagayo, take to your trampers. Vineyards and
Dancing John is the word. Am I comprehended?

GYPSIES
Ay! ay!

CRUZADO
Away, then!

[Exeunt **SEVERALLY**. **CRUZADO** walks up the stage, and disappears among the trees. Enter **PRECIOSA**.

PRECIOSA
How strangely gleams through the gigantic trees
The red light of the forge! Wild, beckoning shadows
Stalk through the forest, ever and anon
Rising and bending with the flickering flame,
Then flitting into darkness! So within me
Strange hopes and fears do beckon to each other,
My brightest hopes giving dark fears a being
As the light does the shadow. Woe is me
How still it is about me, and how lonely!

[**BARTOLOME** rushes in.

BARTOLOME
Ho! Preciosa!

PRECIOSA
O Bartolome!

Thou here?

BARTOLOME
Lo! I am here.

PRECIOSA
Whence comest thou?

BARTOLOME
From the rough ridges of the wild Sierra,
From caverns in the rocks, from hunger, thirst,
And fever! Like a wild wolf to the sheepfold.
Come I for thee, my lamb.

PRECIOSA
O touch me not!
The Count of Lara's blood is on thy hands!
The Count of Lara's curse is on thy soul!
Do not come near me! Pray, begone from here
Thou art in danger! They have set a price
Upon thy head!

BARTOLOME
Ay, and I've wandered long
Among the mountains; and for many days
Have seen no human face, save the rough swineherd's.
The wind and rain have been my sole companions.
I shouted to them from the rocks thy name,
And the loud echo sent it back to me,
Till I grew mad. I could not stay from thee,
And I am here! Betray me, if thou wilt.

PRECIOSA
Betray thee? I betray thee?

BARTOLOME
Preciosa!
I come for thee! for thee I thus brave death!
Fly with me o'er the borders of this realm!
Fly with me!

PRECIOSA
Speak of that no more. I cannot.
I'm thine no longer.

BARTOLOME
O, recall the time
When we were children! how we played together,

How we grew up together; how we plighted
Our hearts unto each other, even in childhood!
Fulfil thy promise, for the hour has come.
I'm hunted from the kingdom, like a wolf!
Fulfil thy promise.

PRECIOSA
'T was my father's promise.
Not mine. I never gave my heart to thee,
Nor promised thee my hand!

BARTOLOME
False tongue of woman!
And heart more false!

PRECIOSA
Nay, listen unto me.
I will speak frankly. I have never loved thee;
I cannot love thee. This is not my fault,
It is my destiny. Thou art a man
Restless and violent. What wouldst thou with me,
A feeble girl, who have not long to live,
Whose heart is broken? Seek another wife,
Better than I, and fairer; and let not
Thy rash and headlong moods estrange her from thee.
Thou art unhappy in this hopeless passion,
I never sought thy love; never did aught
To make thee love me. Yet I pity thee,
And most of all I pity thy wild heart,
That hurries thee to crimes and deeds of blood,
Beware, beware of that.

BARTOLOME
For thy dear sake
I will be gentle. Thou shalt teach me patience.

PRECIOSA
Then take this farewell, and depart in peace.
Thou must not linger here.

BARTOLOME
Come, come with me.

PRECIOSA
Hark! I hear footsteps.

BARTOLOME
I entreat thee, come!

PRECIOSA
Away! It is in vain.

BARTOLOME
Wilt thou not come?

PRECIOSA
Never!

BARTOLOME
Then woe, eternal woe, upon thee!
Thou shalt not be another's. Thou shalt die.

[Exit.

PRECIOSA
All holy angels keep me in this hour!
Spirit of her who bore me, look upon me!
Mother of God, the glorified, protect me!
Christ and the saints, be merciful unto me!
Yet why should I fear death? What is it to die?
To leave all disappointment, care, and sorrow,
To leave all falsehood, treachery, and unkindness,
All ignominy, suffering, and despair,
And be at rest forever! O dull heart,
Be of good cheer! When thou shalt cease to beat,
Then shalt thou cease to suffer and complain!

[Enter **VICTORIAN** and **HYPOLITO** behind.

VICTORIAN
'T is she! Behold, how beautiful she stands
Under the tent-like trees!

HYPOLITO
A woodland nymph!

VICTORIAN
I pray thee, stand aside. Leave me.

HYPOLITO
Be wary.
Do not betray thyself too soon.

VICTORIAN [Disguising his voice]
Hist! Gypsy!

PRECIOSA [Aside, with emotion]
That voice! that voice from heaven! O speak again!
Who is it calls?

VICTORIAN
A friend.

PRECIOSA [Aside]
'T is he! 'T is he!
I thank thee, Heaven, that thou hast heard my prayer,
And sent me this protector! Now be strong,
Be strong, my heart! I must dissemble here.
False friend or true?

VICTORIAN
A true friend to the true;
Fear not; come hither. So; can you tell fortunes?

PRECIOSA
Not in the dark. Come nearer to the fire.
Give me your hand. It is not crossed, I see.

VICTORIAN [Putting a piece of gold into her hand]
There is the cross.

PRECIOSA
Is 't silver?

VICTORIAN
No, 't is gold.

PRECIOSA
There's a fair lady at the Court, who loves you,
And for yourself alone.

VICTORIAN
Fie! the old story!
Tell me a better fortune for my money;
Not this old woman's tale!

PRECIOSA
You are passionate;
And this same passionate humor in your blood
Has marred your fortune. Yes; I see it now;
The line of life is crossed by many marks.
Shame! shame! O you have wronged the maid who loved you!
How could you do it?

VICTORIAN
I never loved a maid;
For she I loved was then a maid no more.

PRECIOSA
How know you that?

VICTORIAN
A little bird in the air
Whispered the secret.

PRECIOSA
There, take back your gold!
Your hand is cold, like a deceiver's hand!
There is no blessing in its charity!
Make her your wife, for you have been abused;
And you shall mend your fortunes, mending hers.

VICTORIAN [Aside]
How like an angel's speaks the tongue of woman,
When pleading in another's cause her own!
That is a pretty ring upon your finger.
Pray give it me.

[Tries to take the ring.

PRECIOSA
No; never from my hand
Shall that be taken!

VICTORIAN
Why, 't is but a ring.
I'll give it back to you; or, if I keep it,
Will give you gold to buy you twenty such.

PRECIOSA
Why would you have this ring?

VICTORIAN
A traveller's fancy,
A whim, and nothing more. I would fain keep it
As a memento of the Gypsy camp
In Guadarrama, and the fortune-teller
Who sent me back to wed a widowed maid.
Pray, let me have the ring.

PRECIOSA
No, never! never!

I will not part with it, even when I die;
But bid my nurse fold my pale fingers thus,
That it may not fall from them. 'T is a token
Of a beloved friend, who is no more.

VICTORIAN
How? dead?

PRECIOSA
Yes; dead to me; and worse than dead.
He is estranged! And yet I keep this ring.
I will rise with it from my grave hereafter,
To prove to him that I was never false.

VICTORIAN [Aside]
Be still, my swelling heart! one moment, still!
Why, 't is the folly of a love-sick girl.
Come, give it me, or I will say 't is mine,
And that you stole it.

PRECIOSA
O, you will not dare
To utter such a falsehood!

VICTORIAN
I not dare?
Look in my face, and say if there is aught
I have not dared, I would not dare for thee!

[She rushes into his arms.

PRECIOSA
'T is thou! 't is thou! Yes; yes; my heart's elected!
My dearest-dear Victorian! my soul's heaven!
Where hast thou been so long? Why didst thou leave me?

VICTORIAN
Ask me not now, my dearest Preciosa.
Let me forget we ever have been parted!

PRECIOSA
Hadst thou not come—

VICTORIAN
I pray thee, do not chide me!

PRECIOSA
I should have perished here among these Gypsies.

VICTORIAN
Forgive me, sweet! for what I made thee suffer.
Think'st thou this heart could feel a moment's joy,
Thou being absent? O, believe it not!
Indeed, since that sad hour I have not slept,
For thinking of the wrong I did to thee
Dost thou forgive me? Say, wilt thou forgive me?

PRECIOSA
I have forgiven thee. Ere those words of anger
Were in the book of Heaven writ down against thee,
I had forgiven thee.

VICTORIAN
I'm the veriest fool
That walks the earth, to have believed thee false.
It was the Count of Lara—

PRECIOSA
That bad man
Has worked me harm enough. Hast thou not heard—

VICTORIAN
I have heard all. And yet speak on, speak on!
Let me but hear thy voice, and I am happy;
For every tone, like some sweet incantation,
Calls up the buried past to plead for me.
Speak, my beloved, speak into my heart,
Whatever fills and agitates thine own.

[They walk aside.

HYPOLITO
All gentle quarrels in the pastoral poets,
All passionate love scenes in the best romances,
All chaste embraces on the public stage,
All soft adventures, which the liberal stars
Have winked at, as the natural course of things,
Have been surpassed here by my friend, the student,
And this sweet Gypsy lass, fair Preciosa!

PRECIOSA
Senor Hypolito! I kiss your hand.
Pray, shall I tell your fortune?

HYPOLITO
Not to-night;

For, should you treat me as you did Victorian,
And send me back to marry maids forlorn,
My wedding day would last from now till Christmas.

CHISPA [Within]
What ho! the Gypsies, ho! Beltran Cruzado!
Halloo! halloo! halloo! halloo!

[Enters booted, with a whip and lantern.

VICTORIAN
What now
Why such a fearful din? Hast thou been robbed?

CHISPA
Ay, robbed and murdered; and good evening to you,
My worthy masters.

VICTORIAN
Speak; what brings thee here?

CHISPA [To **PRECIOSA**]
Good news from Court; good news! Beltran Cruzado,
The Count of the Cales, is not your father,
But your true father has returned to Spain
Laden with wealth. You are no more a Gypsy.

VICTORIAN
Strange as a Moorish tale!

CHISPA
And we have all
Been drinking at the tavern to your health,
As wells drink in November, when it rains.

VICTORIAN
Where is the gentlemen?

CHISPA
As the old song says,
His body is in Segovia,
His soul is in Madrid,

PRECIOSA
Is this a dream? O, if it be a dream,
Let me sleep on, and do not wake me yet!
Repeat thy story! Say I'm not deceived!
Say that I do not dream! I am awake;

This is the Gypsy camp; this is Victorian,
And this his friend, Hypolito! Speak! speak!
Let me not wake and find it all a dream!

VICTORIAN
It is a dream, sweet child! a waking dream,
A blissful certainty, a vision bright
Of that rare happiness, which even on earth
Heaven gives to those it loves. Now art thou rich,
As thou wast ever beautiful and good;
And I am now the beggar.

PRECIOSA [Giving him her hand]
I have still
A hand to give.

CHISPA [Aside]
And I have two to take.
I've heard my grandmother say, that Heaven gives almonds
To those who have no teeth. That's nuts to crack,
I've teeth to spare, but where shall I find almonds?

VICTORIAN
What more of this strange story?

CHISPA
Nothing more.
Your friend, Don Carlos, is now at the village
Showing to Pedro Crespo, the Alcalde,
The proofs of what I tell you. The old hag,
Who stole you in your childhood, has confessed;
And probably they'll hang her for the crime,
To make the celebration more complete.

VICTORIAN
No; let it be a day of general joy;
Fortune comes well to all, that comes not late.
Now let us join Don Carlos.

HYPOLITO
So farewell,
The student's wandering life! Sweet serenades,
Sung under ladies' windows in the night,
And all that makes vacation beautiful!
To you, ye cloistered shades of Alcala,
To you, ye radiant visions of romance,
Written in books, but here surpassed by truth,
The Bachelor Hypolito returns,

And leaves the Gypsy with the Spanish Student.

A **MULETEER** crosses the stage, sitting sideways on his mule and lighting a paper cigar with flint and steel.

SONG.

If thou art sleeping, maiden,
Awake and open thy door,
'T is the break of day, and we must away,
O'er meadow, and mount, and moor.

Wait not to find thy slippers,
But come with thy naked feet;
We shall have to pass through the dewy grass,
And waters wide and fleet.

[Disappears down the pass. Enter a **MONK**. A **SHEPHERD** appears on the rocks above.

MONK
Ave Maria, gratia plena. Ola! good man!

SHEPHERD
Ola!

MONK
Is this the road to Segovia?

SHEPHERD
It is, your reverence.

MONK
How far is it?

SHEPHERD
I do not know.

MONK
What is that yonder in the valley?

SHEPHERD
San Ildefonso.

MONK

A long way to breakfast.

SHEPHERD
Ay, marry.

MONK
Are there robbers in these mountains?

SHEPHERD
Yes, and worse than that.

MONK
What?

SHEPHERD
Wolves.

MONK
Santa Maria! Come with me to San Ildefonso, and thou shalt be well rewarded.

SHEPHERD
What wilt thou give me?

MONK
An Agnus Dei and my benediction.

[They disappear. A mounted **CONTRABANDISTA** passes, wrapped in his cloak, and a gun at his saddle-bow. He goes down the pass singing.

SONG.

Worn with speed is my good steed,
And I march me hurried, worried;
Onward, caballito mio,
With the white star in thy forehead!
Onward, for here comes the Ronda,
And I hear their rifles crack!
Ay, jaleo! Ay, ay, jaleo!
Ay, jaleo! They cross our track.

[Song dies away. Enter **PRECIOSA**, on horseback, attended by **VICTORIAN**, **HYPOLITO**, **DON CARLOS**, and **CHISPA**, on foot, and armed.

VICTORIAN
This is the highest point. Here let us rest.
See, Preciosa, see how all about us
Kneeling, like hooded friars, the misty mountains
Receive the benediction of the sun!

O glorious sight!

PRECIOSA
Most beautiful indeed!

HYPOLITO
Most wonderful!

VICTORIAN
And in the vale below,
Where yonder steeples flash like lifted halberds,
San Ildefonso, from its noisy belfries,
Sends up a salutation to the morn,
As if an army smote their brazen shields,
And shouted victory!

PRECIOSA
And which way lies Segovia?

VICTORIAN
At a great distance yonder.
Dost thou not see it?

PRECIOSA
No. I do not see it.

VICTORIAN
The merest flaw that dents the horizon's edge.
There, yonder!

HYPOLITO
'T is a notable old town,
Boasting an ancient Roman aqueduct,
And an Alcazar, builded by the Moors,
Wherein, you may remember, poor Gil Blas
Was fed on Pan del Rey. O, many a time
Out of its grated windows have I looked
Hundreds of feet plumb down to the Eresma,
That, like a serpent through the valley creeping,
Glides at its foot.

PRECIOSA
O yes! I see it now,
Yet rather with my heart than with mine eyes,
So faint it is. And all my thoughts sail thither,
Freighted with prayers and hopes, and forward urged
Against all stress of accident, as in
The Eastern Tale, against the wind and tide

Great ships were drawn to the Magnetic Mountains,
And there were wrecked, and perished in the sea!

[She weeps.

VICTORIAN
O gentle spirit! Thou didst bear unmoved
Blasts of adversity and frosts of fate!
But the first ray of sunshine that falls on thee
Melts thee to tears! O, let thy weary heart
Lean upon mine! and it shall faint no more,
Nor thirst, nor hunger; but be comforted
And filled with my affection.

PRECIOSA
Stay no longer!
My father waits. Methinks I see him there,
Now looking from the window, and now watching
Each sound of wheels or footfall in the street,
And saying, "Hark! she comes!" O father! father!

[They descend the pass. **CHISPA** remains behind.

CHISPA
I have a father, too, but he is a dead one. Alas and alack-a-day. Poor was I born, and poor do I remain. I
neither win nor lose. Thus I was, through the world, half the time on foot, and the other half walking;
and always as merry as a thunder-storm in the night. And so we plough along, as the fly said to the ox.
Who knows what may happen? Patience, and shuffle the cards! I am not yet so bald that you can see
my brains; and perhaps, after all, I shall some day go to Rome, and come back Saint Peter. Benedicite!

[Exit.

[A pause. Then enter **BARTOLOME** wildly, as if in pursuit, with a carbine in his hand.

BARTOLOME
They passed this way! I hear their horses' hoofs!
Yonder I see them! Come, sweet caramillo,
This serenade shall be the Gypsy's last!

[Fires down the pass.

Ha! ha! Well whistled, my sweet caramillo!
Well whistled!—I have missed her!—O my God!

[The shot is returned. **BARTOLOME** falls.

Henry Wadsworth Longfellow was born on February 27th, 1807 in Portland, Maine (then part of Massachusetts) to Stephen Longfellow and Zilpah (nee Wadsworth) Longfellow. His father was a lawyer, and his maternal grandfather, Peleg Wadsworth, was a general in the American Revolutionary War and a Member of Congress.

It was a large family. Longfellow was the second of eight children; his siblings were Stephen (1805), Elizabeth (1808), Anne (1810), Alexander (1814), Mary (1816), Ellen (1818) and Samuel (1819).

Longfellow attended a dame school at the age of three and by age six was enrolled at the private Portland Academy. He was very studious and quickly became fluent in Latin. His mother encouraged his love of reading and learning and introduced him to many literary classics.

He published his first poem, a patriotic four-stanza affair entitled "The Battle of Lovell's Pond", in the Portland Gazette on November 17, 1820. He remained at the Portland Academy until he was fourteen. As a child, he spent much of his summers at his grandfather Peleg's farm in the nearby town of Hiram.

In the fall of 1822, the 15-year-old Longfellow enrolled at Bowdoin College in Brunswick, Maine. His grandfather was a founder of the college and his father a trustee. Here he met and befriended Nathaniel Hawthorne. Longfellow was already thinking of a career in literature. In his senior year he wrote to his father: "I will not disguise it in the least... the fact is, I most eagerly aspire after future eminence in literature, my whole soul burns most ardently after it, and every earthly thought centers in it... I am almost confident in believing, that if I can ever rise in the world it must be by the exercise of my talents in the wide field of literature."

Poetry was the writing form he felt most at ease with and he offered poems to many newspapers and magazines. Between January 1824 and graduation in 1825, he had almost 40 poems published, over half of which were in the short-lived Boston periodical The United States Literary Gazette.

When Longfellow graduated, he was ranked a pleasing fourth in the class, and had been elected to Phi Beta Kappa. He was quickly offered the post of professor of modern languages at his alma mater.

Accounts suggest that part of the requirement of acceptance was to tour Europe to become more immersed in both languages and cultures. Longfellow began his tour of Europe in May 1826 aboard the ship Cadmus. His travels in Europe would last three years and cost his father the princely sum of $2,604.24. He visited France, Spain, Italy, Germany and England before returning to the United States in mid-August 1829.

His stock of languages now included French, Spanish, Portuguese, and German, and impressively, mostly without any formal instruction.

On August 27th, 1829, he wrote to the president of Bowdoin that he was turning down the professorship because he considered the $600 salary "disproportionate to the duties required". The trustees countered by raising the salary to $800 and an additional $100 to serve as the college's librarian, a post which required only one hour's attention a day.

On September 14th, 1831, Longfellow married Mary Storer Potter, a childhood friend from Portland. The couple settled in Brunswick. Longfellow now published several non-fiction and fiction prose pieces inspired by his friend Washington Irving, whom he had met in Madrid during his travels, these included "The Indian Summer" and "The Bald Eagle" in 1833.

During his years teaching at the college, he translated textbooks in French, Italian and Spanish; his first published book was in 1833, a translation of the poetry of the medieval Spanish poet Jorge Manrique. A travel book, Outre-Mer: A Pilgrimage Beyond the Sea, was first published in serial form before a book edition in 1835.

In December 1834, Longfellow received a letter from Josiah Quincy III, president of Harvard College, offering him the Smith Professorship of Modern Languages with the condition that he first spend a year or so abroad. The Longfellow's set off for Europe. He would now be able to add German, Dutch, Danish, Swedish, Finnish, and Icelandic to his repertoire of languages.

During the trip they discovered that Mary was pregnant. Sadly, in October 1835, she miscarried some six months into the pregnancy. Then followed several weeks of illness and at the age of 22 on November 29th, 1835 she died. Longfellow had her body embalmed, placed in a lead coffin itself inside an oak coffin which was then shipped to Mount Auburn Cemetery near Boston. He wrote movingly "One thought occupies me night and day... She is dead—She is dead! All day I am weary and sad".

Back in the United States, Longfellow took up the professorship at Harvard. He was required to live in Cambridge, close to the campus and rented rooms at the Craigie House in the spring of 1837. The home, built in 1759, had once been the headquarters of George Washington during the Siege of Boston.

Longfellow now felt able to publish again, starting with the collection Voices of the Night in 1839. It was mainly comprised of translations together with nine original poems and seven poems written back in his teenage years.

His romantic interests also began to surface again. He had begun to court Frances 'Fanny' Appleton, daughter of the Boston industrialist Nathan Appleton. At first, the independent-minded Appleton was not interested in marriage but Longfellow was determined. In July 1839, he wrote to a friend: "Victory hangs doubtful. The lady says she will not! I say she shall! It is not pride, but the madness of passion".

In late 1839, Longfellow published Hyperion, a book in prose inspired by his trips abroad and his still un-successful courtship of Fanny Appleton. Amidst this, Longfellow fell into "periods of neurotic depression with moments of panic" and required a six-month leave of absence from Harvard to attend a health spa in the former Marienberg Benedictine Convent at Boppard in Germany.

Ballads and Other Poems was published in 1841 and included "The Village Blacksmith" and "The Wreck of the Hesperus". His reputation as a poet, and a commercial one at that, was set.

Longfellow published a play in 1842, The Spanish Student, based on his memories from his time in Spain in the 1820s. A small collection, Poems on Slavery, was also published in 1842. This was Longfellow's first public support of abolitionism. However, as Longfellow himself said, the poems were "so mild that even a Slaveholder might read them without losing his appetite for breakfast". The New England Anti-Slavery Association, however, was satisfied enough with the intent of the collection to reprint it for their own distribution.

On May 10th, 1843, after seven years in pursuit, Longfellow received a letter from Fanny Appleton agreeing to marry him. He was elated and immediately walked 90 minutes to meet her at her house.

Nathan Appleton bought the Craigie House as a wedding present to the pair. Longfellow lived there for the rest of his life. His love for Fanny is evident from Longfellow's only love poem, the sonnet "The Evening Star", written in October 1845:

"O my beloved, my sweet Hesperus!
My morning and my evening star of love!"

He once attended a ball without her and said, "The lights seemed dimmer, the music sadder, the flowers fewer, and the women less fair."

Longfellow and Fanny had six children: Charles Appleton (1844), Ernest Wadsworth (1845), Fanny (1847, who died in infancy), Alice Mary (1850), Edith (1853), and Anne Allegra (1855).

Aware of his growing stature and his ability to influence others he also encouraged and supported many other translators. In 1845, he published The Poets and Poetry of Europe, a large 800-page compendium of translated works by other writers. Longfellow intended the anthology "to bring together, into a compact and convenient form, as large an amount as possible of those English translations which are scattered through many volumes, and are not accessible to the general reader".

On November 1st, 1847, the epic poem Evangeline was published.

Longfellow's literary income was now becoming quite substantial: in 1840, he had made $219 but by 1850 it had grown to a very promising $1,900.

On June 14th, 1853, Longfellow held a farewell dinner party at his Cambridge home for his great friend Nathaniel Hawthorne, who was preparing to move overseas.

In 1854, Longfellow retired from Harvard, devoting himself entirely to writing. He would be awarded an honorary doctorate of laws from Harvard in 1859.

The Song of Haiwatha, his epic poem, and perhaps his best known and enjoyed work was published in 1855.

On a hot July 9th day, 1861, Fanny was putting several locks of her children's hair into an envelope and making attempts to seal it with hot sealing wax while Longfellow took a nap. The circumstances of what happened next vary but the actuality is that Fanny's dress caught fire. Her screams awakened Longfellow who rushed to help her and threw a rug over her and stifled the flames with his own body as best he could, but Fanny was already horrifically burned.

A doctor was called and Fanny was taken to her room to recover. She was in and out of consciousness throughout the night and was also administered ether. The next morning, July 10th, 1861, she died shortly after 10 o'clock after asking for a cup of coffee.

Longfellow, in his effort to save her had also been badly burned and was unable to attend her funeral. His facial injuries required he stopped shaving. The ensuing beard now became the quintessential look that everyone remembers from pictures.

Devastated, he never fully recovered and sometimes resorted to laudanum and ether to ease the pain. He worried he would go insane and begged "not to be sent to an asylum" and noted that he was "inwardly bleeding to death". In the sonnet "The Cross of Snow" (1879), which he wrote eighteen years later he wrote:

"Such is the cross I wear upon my breast
These eighteen years, through all the changing scenes
And seasons, changeless since the day she died".

Longfellow spent several years translating Dante Alighieri's epic poem, The Divine Comedy. To aid him in perfecting the translation and reviewing proofs, he invited several friends to weekly meetings every Wednesday from 1864. This became known as the "Dante Club", and regulars included William Dean Howells, James Russell Lowell, Charles Eliot Norton and other occasional guests. The full three-volume translation was published in the spring of 1867, though Longfellow would continue to revise it. It was wildly popular and was re-printed four times in its first year.

By 1868, Longfellow's annual income was over a staggering $48,000.

Longfellow was also part of a group of Poets who became known as The Fireside Poets. The group included Longfellow, William Cullen Bryant, John Greenleaf Whittier, James Russell Lowell, and Oliver Wendell Holmes Snr. Occasionally Ralph Waldo Emerson is also placed among their number. The name "Fireside Poets" derives from poetry reading as a collective family entertainment of the times.

During the 1860s, Longfellow, still a committed abolitionist, also hoped for a coming together, a reconciliation, between the north and south after the dark days of the Civil War. When his son was wounded during the war, he wrote the poem "Christmas Bells", later the basis of the carol I Heard the Bells on Christmas Day.

In 1874, Samuel Cutler Ward helped him sell the poem "The Hanging of the Crane" to the New York Ledger for $3,000; it was the highest price ever paid for a poem. An astonishing sum. But Longfellow was worth it. His fame and audience were widespread and devoted.

Continuing in his hopes for a better and more united America he wrote in his journal in 1878: "I have only one desire; and that is for harmony, and a frank and honest understanding between North and South". Longfellow, despite his aversion to public speaking, took up an offer from Joshua Chamberlain to speak at his fiftieth reunion at Bowdoin College. Here he read the poem "Morituri Salutamus" so quietly that few could hear.

On August 22th, 1879, a female admirer who seemed to know little about his history, traveled to Longfellow's house in Cambridge and, unaware to whom she was speaking, asked Longfellow: "Is this the house where Longfellow was born?" Longfellow told her it was not. The visitor then asked if he had died here. "Not yet", he replied.

Much of Longfellow's work is recognized for its melody-like musicality. As he says, "what a writer asks of his reader is not so much to like as to listen".

Longfellow, like many others of the period, called for the development of high quality American literature. In his work, Kavanagh, a character says: "We want a national literature commensurate with our mountains and rivers... We want a national epic that shall correspond to the size of the country... We want a national drama in which scope shall be given to our gigantic ideas and to the unparalleled activity of our people... In a word, we want a national literature altogether shaggy and unshorn, that shall shake the earth, like a herd of buffaloes thundering over the prairies."

As a translator Longfellow was very impressive. His translation of Dante's The Divine Comedy became a requirement for those who wanted to be a part of high culture.

In 1874, Longfellow oversaw a 31-volume anthology called Poems of Places, collecting poems of several geographical locations; Europe, Asia, and the Arabian countries. It was a work of great educational endeavor but Emerson was disappointed and is said to have told Longfellow: "The world is expecting better things of you than this... You are wasting time that should be bestowed upon original production".

At this point in his life Longfellow could look back and see that his early collections, Voices of the Night and Ballads and Other Poems, had made him instantly popular. The New-Yorker called him "one of the very few in our time who has successfully aimed in putting poetry to its best and sweetest uses". The Southern Literary Messenger immediately put Longfellow "among the first of our American poets".

The rapidity with which American readers embraced Longfellow was unparalleled in publishing history in the United States. His popularity spread throughout Europe, his poems translated into Italian, French, German, and other languages.

Longfellow was the most popular poet of his day. As a friend once wrote to him, "no other poet was so fully recognized in his lifetime". Some of his works including "Paul Revere's Ride" and "The Song of Haiwatha" may have rewritten the facts but became essential parts of the American psyche and culture. He was so admired that on his 70th birthday in 1877 the atmosphere was that of a national holiday, with parades, speeches, and, of course, the reading of his poems.

Over the years, Longfellow's reputation came to include his personality; he was a gentle, placid, poetic soul. James Russell Lowell said, Longfellow had an "absolute sweetness, simplicity, and modesty". The reality was that Longfellow's life was much more difficult than was assumed. He suffered from neuralgia, which caused him constant pain, and poor eyesight. The difficulties of coping with the loss of two wives also took its toll. He was very quiet, reserved, and private; in later years, he became increasingly unsocial and avoided leaving home if he could.

In March 1882, Longfellow went to bed with severe stomach pain. He endured the pain for several days with the help of opium.

Henry Wadsworth Longfellow died, surrounded by family, on Friday, March 24th, 1882. He had been suffering from peritonitis.

He is buried with both of his wives at Mount Auburn Cemetery in Cambridge, Massachusetts. At Longfellow's funeral, his friend Ralph Waldo Emerson called him "a sweet and beautiful soul".

At the time of his death, his estate was valued at $356,320.

In 1884, Longfellow became the first non-British writer for whom a sculpted bust was placed in Poet's Corner of Westminster Abbey in London; he remains the sole American poet thus represented.

Henry Wadsworth Longfellow – A Concise Bibliography

Outre-Mer: A Pilgrimage Beyond the Sea (Travelogue) (1835)
Hyperion, a Romance (1839)
The Spanish Student. A Play in Three Acts (1843)
Evangeline: A Tale of Acadie (poem) (1847)
Kavanagh (1849)
The Golden Legend (poem) (1851)
The Song of Hiawatha (poem) (1855)
The New England Tragedies (1868)
The Divine Tragedy (1871)
Christus: A Mystery (1872)
Aftermath (poem) (1873)
The Arrow and the Song (poem)

Poetry Collections

Voices of the Night (1839)
Ballads & Other Poems (1841)
Poems on Slavery (1842)
The Belfry of Bruges & Other Poems (1845)
The Seaside and the Fireside (1850)
The Poetical Works of Henry Wadsworth Longfellow (1852)
The Courtship of Miles Standish & Other Poems (1858)
Tales of a Wayside Inn (1863)
Birds of Passage (1863)
Household Poems (1865)
Flower-de-Luce (1867)
Three Books of Song (1872)
The Masque of Pandora & Other Poems (1875)
Kéramos & Other Poems (1878)
Ultima Thule (1880)
In the Harbor (1882)
Michel Angelo: A Fragment (incomplete; published posthumously)

Translations

Coplas de Don Jorge Manrique (Translation from Spanish) (1833)
Dante's Divine Comedy (Translation) (1867)

Anthologies

Poets and Poetry of Europe (Translations) (1845)
The Waif (1845)
Poems of Places (1874)